The
MAIN ST
Moment

The
MAIN STREET
Moment

Fighting Back to Save
the American Dream

Gerald W. McEntee *&* Lee Saunders

NATION
BOOKS

New York
www.nationbooks.org

Copyright © 2012 by The American Federation
of State, County and Municipal Employees

All proceeds from sales of this book will be donated to the AFSCME Fallen Heroes
Fund. To donate to the fund, visit: www.afscme.org/fund.

Published by Nation Books, a Member of the Perseus Books Group
116 East 16th Street, 8th floor
New York, NY 10003-2112

Nation Books is a co-publishing venture of the Nation Institute
and the Perseus Books Group.

Books published by Nation Books are available at special discounts for bulk
purchases in the United States by corporations, institutions, and other organizations.
For more information, please contact the Special Markets Department at the
Perseus Books Group, 2300 Chestnut Street, Suite 200, Philadelphia, PA 19103-
4331, or call (800) 810-4145, ext. 5000, or e-mail
special.markets@perseusbooks.com.

Editorial production by *Marra*thon Production Services. www.marrathon.net

Design by Jane Raese

A CIP catalog record for this book is available from the Library of Congress.

ISBN 978-1-56858-721-9 (paperback)
ISBN 978-1-56858-722-6 (e-book)

10 9 8 7 6 5 4 3 2 1

DEDICATED TO OUR 1.6 MILLION SISTERS AND BROTHERS

WHO MAKE AMERICA HAPPEN

Contents

Preface

The electoral debacle of 2010—where corporate-backed politicians stormed Congress and state capitals across the country—opened the door to the greatest onslaught against working people since the emergence of the robber barons of the late nineteenth century. Seizing upon the frustration of average citizens still reeling from an economic crisis that had threatened their jobs and retirement security, these elected officials pursued a divide-and-conquer strategy that almost worked, that—if we are not diligent—may yet still work. Multimillionaire media moguls and talking heads stoked the flames of desperation with a barrage of anti-government rhetoric that seemed, merely by repetition, to reflect reality. In Washington, D.C., the new majority in the House of Representatives passed a budget that took a wrecking ball to the very pillars of the American Dream, including Medicare, Social Security, education assistance, health research, and job training programs.

In dozens of states, radical politicians, in debt to the corporate interests that fund their campaigns, launched an all-out assault on the working middle class—through unnecessary cuts in health and education programs, privatization schemes, and corrupt efforts to turn the public purse over to profiteers out to make a buck at the taxpayers' expense.

In Wisconsin and Ohio, the politicians also targeted the very freedom of workers to have a voice on the job.

This new breed of radical politicians across the country has no doubt succeeded in pushing through policies that will have damning and lasting impact on the American Dream, including denying union rights, voter suppression, and selling off public services to the highest corporate bidders. But they have also sparked an opposing, passionate, energized, and focused movement that continues to grow as we write today. It is a movement that won a moral victory in Wisconsin, an electoral victory in Ohio, and is on the march to save the American Dream this fall and beyond.

This book is our effort to take stock of this Main Street moment. From coast to coast, Americans have mobilized, rallied, lobbied, and protested in vast numbers, building the foundation for an ever-expanding coalition of millions, committed to addressing the growing crisis of economic inequality and the disastrous record of the 1 percent during the past thirty years.

We tell the story of how this happened, along with a look at how power—political power as well as economic power—has shifted during the past thirty years into the hands of the wealthiest members of our society. Wall Street and the billionaires didn't get this powerful by accident. They planned for it. They paid for it. And they will not give up power and restore our democracy to the people without a fight.

This book is not an attack on capitalism, success, or wealth. But at the core of this book is a belief that, increasingly, we are living in a society where the cards are marked. It is not a belief one comes to easily or with any degree of satisfaction. And it is a belief that is supported, sadly, by the facts. One of the tenets of the American Dream—class mobility—now appears too far out of reach for too many Americans.

And yet . . .

The spirit kindled in Madison and Columbus has now spread throughout America, in state capitals, in workplaces and campus halls, in houses of worship and senior centers, in schools and veterans' halls. Finally, with a burst of energy, we saw the spirit inspire "Occupy Wall Street," the remarkable protest movement that has done so much to call attention to the criminal inequality that currently exists in our nation. It is not too much to hope that we are witnessing the early hours of nothing less than the dawn of a new day, when an invigorated and inspired coalition of workers, students, clergy, small-business owners, and others can all come together to say, "Enough is enough."

As democratically elected officers of a national union of public service employees, we represent members in communities across America—plowing streets, caring for the ill, looking after children and the elderly, working in schools, hospitals, and prisons. They are active in politics because they know what is at stake for communities when the wrong people are elected into office. This, fundamentally, is why they are under attack. Corporations, Wall Street moneymen, and the politicians who work for them know that public service workers and their unions are the last line of defense against their culture of greed.

Public service workers believe in public service, not in survival of the fittest. They believe that we are all in this together. You will meet some of them in the pages that follow. They believe in a country where we find solutions based on basic

American values, rather than the law of the jungle. They know that if we lose, the American Dream dies, replaced by a national Darwinian nightmare in which only a chosen few survive. They are what Main Street looks like. They are what democracy looks like.

We stand at a crossroads. We can either continue down the path of greater income inequality, ceding our voices and our democracy to the wealthy and the powerful. Or we can fight back. That is what men and women across America have chosen to do to make this Main Street's moment. They chose to fight and to build a better future—for themselves, for their communities, and for this country that we love. We have written this book to enlist even more Americans in the struggle to save the soul of our nation and return power once again to the people. We know that, together, we can win this fight.

Acknowledgments

Ernest Hemingway wrote that "there is no friend as loyal as a book." He was wrong. We know that without the help of loyal friends, this book could not have been written. We are enormously grateful for the support and encouragement we received from countless friends and colleagues during the preparation of The Main Street Moment.

Our remarkable wives, Barbara McEntee and Lynne Saunders, have been extraordinarily supportive. We are forever in their debt for their understanding that we have a second family that requires time and attention—AFSCME.

The same debt is owed to our children: McEntee daughters Patricia, Kathy, Kelly and Chris, and their children; Saunders sons Lee, Jr and Ryan. Their patience and support is one of life's true blessings.

We thank the members of AFSCME's International Executive Board for their leadership and support and the remarkable AFSCME leaders in Wisconsin, whose activism in the face of a brutal attack on collective bargaining, set the standard for the whole labor movement. Likewise, our leaders in Ohio, who rallied the citizens of the Buckeye State to overturn Senate Bill 5, and inspired the nation.

We will always appreciate the AFSCME members around the country who told their stories and helped us frame the discussion of the issues. The work they do across the country is essential. They are on the frontlines in the struggle to build a strong middle class and give every person the chance to share in the American Dream. Royalties from this book will go to AFSCME's fallen Heroes Fund, a fund that provides emergency assistance to AFSCME members in their time of need.

The gifted Larry Beinhart brought us his ideas, passion and fresh way of thinking about how to tell this story. This book wouldn't exist without him. Andy Breslau and Carl Bromley of the Nation Institute believed in the importance and timeliness of the project from Day One. Members of the AFSCME Communications Department, notably Chris Policano, Blaine Rummel, Gregory King, Cynthia McCabe and Linda Martin were integral to keeping the book on track. William Wilkinson did a terrific job fact-checking. AFSCME staffers Paul Booth, Jessica Weinstein, Lisa Lindsley, Elissa McBride and Seth Johnson provided informed and invaluable guidance.

Finally, an august group of friends and advisors were generous with their insights: Damon Silvers at the AFL-CIO; Patrick Bresette at DEMOS; Amy Hanauer of Policy Matters Ohio; Brian Rothenberg of Progress Ohio; Larry Mishel of the Economic Policy Institute; Dean Baker of the Center for Economic Policy Research; and Anna Greenberg of Greenberg, Quinlan, Rosner Research.

Thank you all very much for the commitment you have made to making this Main Street's moment.

Where free unions and collective bargaining
are forbidden, freedom is lost.

—RONALD REAGAN
Labor Day speech at Liberty State Park, Jersey City, New Jersey, 1980

CHAPTER ONE

Meet Betty Jean Simmons-Talley

BETTY JEAN SIMMONS-TALLEY is a sixty-four-year-old school bus driver in Columbus, Ohio. Most people call her BJ. She's all of five-foot-four and has a smile that can light up a room.

BJ was born in Alabama. She came north in 1971 because she "didn't want a job that paid the wages of picking cotton." She wanted to be somewhere she would be treated with respect and dignity. And if she had children, somewhere they could get good jobs. Truth be told, it was also because the man she married lived in Ohio.

John Kasich is the fifty-nine-year-old chief of the executive branch of state government in Columbus, Ohio. Kasich was born in McKees Rocks, an old industrial town in Pennsylvania. Kasich likes to describe himself as a "blue-collar guy." Indeed, his father was a mail carrier. His mother was a postal clerk. But Kasich has never worked a blue-collar job himself.[1] Kasich came to Ohio to go to Ohio State, which he graduated from in 1974. He stayed in Ohio, and has had a varied career since, working as a congressman, TV show host, and an investment banker. He was elected governor of Ohio in 2010.

If there are two people who illustrate the issues that go to the heart of this book—the fight for Main Street and the American Dream—it is Betty Jean Simmons-Talley and John Kasich.

In 1979, BJ got a job as a school bus driver. It only paid $3.75 an hour. But she adored the kids and they adored her, so she stayed with it. Wages and benefits have gone up over the years. Now she's making $21.85 an hour. She also gets health care, which is very fortunate because she had cancer a few years ago and her health plan saw her through it. She's now in remission.

BJ will also receive a modest pension when she retires. That's instead of Social Security, which she won't get.

You read that right. Like 30 percent of public employees in America, BJ is not eligible for Social Security: an inconvenient fact that all too often goes unmentioned when politicians rail against public employee pensions. Another fact typically omitted is that 80 percent of a public worker's pension, like the one BJ has, comes from that worker's own contributions and investment returns—not taxpayers.

According to John Kasich and his supporters, BJ's benefits are gold plated. Way over the top. Out of line with what a waitress in a fast-food chain gets. They think she's way overpaid and probably lazy. It's her and her ilk, banded together, who have forced the great state of Ohio to the edge of that abyss called bankruptcy. Not just Ohio, either. A whole bunch of states. Maybe the whole nation. According to politicians like Kasich, BJ and the rest of her bus-driving, floor-mopping,

Courtesy of Allen Zak

street-sweeping, pipe-fixing "thugs," cleaning up after elderly and sick people, teaching young people, and whatever else they claim to do, are the most insidious threat to our fiscal well-being and moral fiber since Ronald Reagan took the Cadillacs away from the welfare queens.

BJ had to be stopped.

Governor Kasich has been a political animal his entire life. In his book *Stand for Something: The Battle for America's Soul*, he said his "childhood goal was to be President of the United States."[2] He majored in political science in college and went around campus telling other kids he was going to be president.

After Kasich graduated he got a job as an administrative assistant to Donald "Buz" Lukens. Buz was a state senator at the time and would later become a congressman. John Kasich would follow the same trajectory.

In 1976, Kasich had run for the Ohio state senate. He was only twenty-six, making him the youngest person ever elected to that office. In 1982, he was elected to Congress. He was a pro-corporate golden boy. In 2000, he gave up his seat and took a shot at what he really wanted: the presidency.

It didn't go well.

As Landon Thomas Jr., reported, "When it came time to take his act to the national level, the pundits begin calling for more gravitas.

"Mr. Kasich snorts. 'The issue was money. M-O-N-E-Y. If I'd had more of that, I would have had all the gravitas'—he fairly spits out the word—'in the world. And you know what? If you look "gravitas" up in the dictionary, it doesn't exist.'"[3]

As the reporter pointed out, *gravitas* is indeed in the dictionary, where it's defined as "a serious and solemn attitude or way of behaving."

Kasich went where all failed pro-corporate golden boys and girls go. He got a show on Fox News. It was called *From the Heartland*.

The M-O-N-E-Y thing apparently really resonated with him, and he went in search of a pile. When he'd been fundraising for his presidential race, he met Richard S. Fuld Jr., chairman and chief executive officer of Lehman Brothers, the fourth-largest investment bank in the United States at the time. According to Kasich, they hit it off. Fuld probably figured he could always find a way to make money with an ex-congressman, and offered Kasich a job with the title of managing director.

"Fuld is an awesome guy," Kasich told the *New York Observer*. "He is the kind of guy you want to go into battle with.

He is a great leader. I like people who are really smart and who are great leaders."[4]

There are others who think differently of Dick Fuld. Before the crash, his nickname was "The Gorilla." After the crash, "Fuld became a symbol of failure, the face of arrogant, blundered, massively overleveraged Wall Street. Fuld is blamed for betting the farm on the way up, then stubbornly refusing to recognize the company's dire straits on the way down."[5] *Time* magazine listed Fuld as one of the "25 People to Blame for the Financial Crisis," noting that he was paid at least half a billion dollars while he nosedived the venerable firm to bankruptcy.[6]

After Lehman tumbled and crumbled into dust, Kasich turned back to what he knew best: politics. He ran for governor of Ohio. Naturally his opponent, incumbent Democratic Governor Ted Strickland, tried to make an issue out of Kasich's stint with Wall Street's kings of chaos and dukes of destruction. So Kasich ran a television ad to play it down. "Here's the truth: I didn't run Lehman Brothers," he said on screen. "I was one of seven hundred managing directors. I worked in a two-man office in Columbus."

Landon Thomas Jr., the reporter for the *New York Observer* who interviewed Kasich in his office, described it a bit differently: "Lehman Brothers managing director John Kasich kicks back in the plush leather chair in his corner office high atop 3 World Financial Center." That's in Manhattan, not Columbus, though he *also* had an office in Columbus where he had two assistants.[7]

You might wonder how much you get paid for working in a two-man office in Columbus. Part time, since he had a show on Fox and was writing books, too.

Many people have asked. Kasich has refused to answer. Except for his last year there, 2008, when Lehman Brothers went bankrupt. Kasich got $587,175 from his part-time job in that little two-man office in Columbus.[8]

The State of Ohio's official website says: "Governor John R. Kasich's top priority is to create jobs." It proudly announces that "Kasich worked as a managing director in the Investment Banking Division of Lehman Brothers, where he helped companies secure the resources they needed to succeed and create jobs." So it's worth noting that Lehman Brothers came in at number nine on another top twenty-five list: "The Layoff Kings, The 25 Companies Responsible for 700,000 Lost Jobs."[9] Their collapse put 23,340 people out of work. That's only counting the direct losses, not the ripple effect on businesses that serviced the company and its employees.

John Kasich got almost $590,000 during the one year we know about: the year Lehman collapsed. What could he have done that was worth it? There's that generic "consulting" mumbo jumbo that we hear about helping companies and creating jobs, but no specifics and no list of programmers, technicians, and warehouse workers hired by anyone. Given that Kasich had never worked in the private sector in his life, it is a fair presumption that his job was really to hit up all his old political pals back home—after all, he'd been in the politics business in Ohio for sixteen years—and sell them Lehman Brothers financial products. As Governor Strickland noted at the time:

In 2002, John Kasich arranged meetings between members of Lehman Brother's private equity department and investment officials at two Ohio Pensions: the Ohio Police

& Fire Pension (OP&F) and the Ohio Public Employees Retirement System (OPERS).

John Kasich claimed he "never approached any other Ohio governmental entity about doing business with Lehman," but new public records information indicates he pitched the State Teacher Retirement System (STRS) on using Lehman as a broker for a real estate investment sale.

The Kasich campaign also claimed he was never involved in direct pitching, but merely made introductions. The public records information indicates Kasich was personally involved with pitching STRS.

Kasich admits that one of his roles at Lehman Brothers was to make introductions and create the potential for future business for the firm. One of the men Kasich introduced to Ohio pensions in 2002 was John Dwyer . . .

Many of the products Dwyer tried to sell involved real estate assets, but standing out from the others was a product Dwyer was personally working on—Lehman's Distressed Structured Credit Fund, which intended to invest heavily in collateralized loan obligations and collateralized debt obligations.

These toxic instruments are widely credited with bringing down Lehman in 2008.[10]

But gubernatorial candidate John Kasich wanted Ohio to forget about those complicated collateralized debt obligations, bankrupt banks, and the crash of 2008. When it came to the State of Ohio, the problem was that school bus driver, BJ Simmons-Talley. She had to be stopped!

Generally speaking, one of the few ways that a school bus driver, a firefighter, a sanitation worker, a street cleaner, or any sort of regular working person can have any sort of power is by being a member of a union. So Governor Kasich decided the only way to set things right was to pass a law that essentially eliminated unions.

Here we hit another peculiarity. Or perhaps a standard hypocrisy.

In *Stand for Something: The Battle for America's Soul*, Kasich leads off with this story:

> A Tee-ball coach . . . was charged with offering one of his eight-year-old players $25 to hit a teammate in the face with a baseball in hopes that the targeted player—a mildly retarded autistic child—would be hurt badly enough to have to leave the game. See . . . all Tee-ballers who show up for their team's game must play at least three innings, and the boy's coach thought this put his team at some kind of disadvantage.
>
> [This] struck me as just about the most unconscionable human act I could imagine—pure evil!—and yet upon reflection I feared it was emblematic of the win-at-all-costs, anything goes mind-set that seems to have taken hold across this great land.[11]

If Kasich felt he was truly battling for America's soul and he really believed that BJ and her union were at the heart of Ohio's economic woes, you would think he'd be the first to call BJ in and talk things over with her. See if some kind of compromise was possible. After all, state workers had taken five pay freezes in nine years, took furloughs, and made compromises on health care. Like almost everyone else, public service workers like BJ were sacrificing to make things better.

Kasich decided that was not the way to go. He came up with a bill that would break BJ's union and then he rammed it through.

That bill—Senate Bill 5 (SB5)—was an attack on the rights and the ability to earn a living of all those people who make the State of Ohio and its cities and towns actually work. But if cops, firefighters, teachers, school janitors, sanitation workers, correctional officers, and the people who keep the water and sewer systems working joined BJ and got enough signatures, they could overturn the law in a citizens' veto.

They called on their families, friends, and neighbors. They stood on corners and they knocked on doors, holding clipboards and ballpoint pens. To fight for their rights and dignity. To retain their shot at the American Dream.

John Kasich had his moment. Now it was Main Street's moment.

But could regular people still beat big money? And how did American workers get forced into this showdown in the first place?

CHAPTER TWO

Special Offer to Our Readers—
$1,500 a Year, for Life

A S A REWARD for getting through Chapter 1, we would like to offer you an extra $1,500 a year for the rest of your working life.

It's really easy.

You want to know how easy? Just live in a state where there are unions. You don't even have to belong to a union. You don't have to support unions. All you have to do is have union members as your neighbors. When you do, the median income in your state, which presumably means your income, will be $1,500 more a year, every year, than that of someone who lives in one of those go-ahead-and-rip-me-off states. They're usually called right-to-work states, but that, like so many of our manufactured labels, is deliberately misleading.

To understand just how misleading it is, look no further than Indiana Governor Mitch Daniels, who rammed through a so-called right-to-work bill this year in the Indiana legislature, claiming it was vital to attract jobs. But as recently as 2006,

Daniels himself admitted such an argument was bogus, saying, "I'm a supporter of the labor laws we have in the state of Indiana and I'm not interested in changing any of them—not the prevailing wage law and certainly not a 'right to work' law. We can succeed in Indiana with the laws we have, respecting the rights of labor and fair and free competition for everyone."[1]

On another level, getting that extra $1,500 is hard.

It's hard because you're up against Wall Street. You're up against the big banks, the pharmaceutical industry, the insurance companies, Fox News (and for that matter, most of the media), and now, apparently, the 2012 version of Mitch Daniels. You're up against the millionaires and billionaires who rent the big-time lawyers and pay the lobbyists and buy our politicians. You're up against the Republican Party and many Democrats, too. You're up against an organized campaign to stop all unions, and since private sector unions have been beaten down to their knees, that campaign is now aimed at public service unions.

But it can be done.

If BJ Simmons-Talley, a woman who drives a school bus in Ohio, can do it, you can, too.

BJ didn't do it alone. She had a union: AFSCME, the American Federation of State, County and Municipal Employees.

AFSCME didn't do it alone.

It was joined by the other public service unions, private sector unions, churches, community groups, small-business owners, and others who understand that a rising tide lifts all boats. And when people have a say and a share in the prosperity they helped produce, America thrives.

We would also like to help you secure your retirement. Whether that's a pension or Social Security, we're sure you want that money to be there when the time comes. You've been making contributions to them and to Medicare, in cash and deferred compensation. You have a right to have those investments pay off.

Who do you think will fight for you, against the companies, in the courts, and in government? Very few organized groups will do so, across the board. First among them are unions.

We're union people. That's on the book cover, so that's no surprise.

You might think that statement is self-serving. We're not saying that unions are the answer to all your financial problems—though we assume an extra $1,500 a year would help—but it is a matter of record that wherever and whenever there are unions, regular people earn more money.

We would also make the claim, and we will substantiate it, that when unions are strong, our economy functions better. It's more productive, it grows faster, and it's more stable. When unions are strong, we don't have crashes and massive bank failures. When we do have recessions, they're shallow and short.

That's a big reason we wrote this book. Unions played a key role in building the middle class, brick by brick. They will play a big role in reviving it. And who better to tell the story of people fighting to save the American Dream than the very folks who see firsthand the devastation that income inequality has wrought? Who better than the employment services worker who sees the anguish in the eyes of her neighbors as they seek jobs when few, if any, exist? Who better than the bus driver who watches as hungry kids board the bus to school every day, clearly affected by their parents' money problems and impending home foreclosure? Who better than the correctional officers who see the impact that privatizing prisons has had on our communities, as profit has trumped public safety?

We won't claim that unions are the only answer to all our problems of income inequality and the quick fix for our economic malaise. That would be foolish and excessive. But they are a vital part of the answer. A necessary element.

As unions are strong, Main Street is strong. As Main Street is strong, the economy is solid and the country is strong. As unions are diminished, we are all diminished. Except for the very richest at the top of the scale, everyone's income goes down. Except for the top 1 percent, everyone's power is diminished, and everyone's voice loses its force.

At this point you may be saying, "Wait a minute! Wait one darn minute! You told me you were going to get me an extra $1,500 a year. Then it turns out it's about living in a union state. But I already live in a union state. So, I feel conned and cheated!"

All right, you people smart enough to live in a union state, we have a deal for you, too!

Though this one you have to work for. Or, if you're lucky, someone else will put in the time and the effort. But, full disclosure, someone does have to work for it.

According to a study by the Center for American Progress Action Fund, "Each percentage point increase in union membership puts about $153 more per year into the pockets of the middle class—meaning that if unionization rates increased by 10 percentage points (to about the level they were in 1980)—then the typical middle class household would earn about $1,500 more this year."[2] That's $1,500 more to go out to dinner now and then, take the kids to the movies, and maybe even get that new refrigerator you've had your eye on, all while investing in and growing your local economy.

Once again, if you're a rugged individualist, or organization averse, let us emphasize that you don't have to be a member of a union to benefit. For example, taking a look at one business, "for a 10% increase in local union densities in the supermarket industry it is estimated that the wages of union employees in that labor market will increase by 5.3% and by 1.2% for non-union."[3] So if you're not in a union, but union membership rises, especially if it's in a profession like your own, yours will likely rise, too.

Let's look at that in reverse for a moment.

Most of our statistics about income distribution are in 20 percent slices of the population. The lowest 20 percent is generally considered the poor. The top 20 percent is the upper class. Though now, with the extreme shifts in wealth, we separate out the top one-tenth of 1 percent of the wealthy from the top 1 percent as the genuine upper class, and everyone below that is sliding down. Still, in most discussions, we look at the group above the lowest 20 percent and below the top 20 percent as the middle class: the employees and residents of Main Street.

In 1968, union membership was close to 30 percent of the workforce. That middle group, representing 60 percent of us, earned 53 percent of the nation's income.

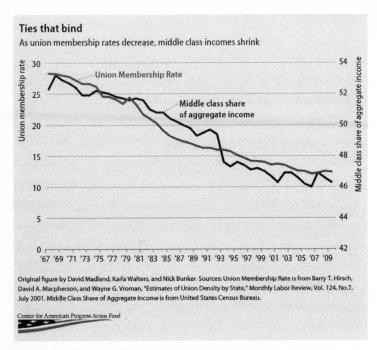

Ties that bind

As union membership rates decrease, middle class incomes shrink

Original figure by David Madland, Karla Walters, and Nick Bunker. Sources: Union Membership Rate is from Barry T. Hirsch, David A. Macpherson, and Wayne G. Vroman, "Estimates of Union Density by State," Monthly Labor Review, Vol. 124, No.7, July 2001. Middle Class Share of Aggregate Income is from United States Census Bureau.

Center for American Progress Action Fund

Source: This material (*Ties that bind*) was created by the Center for American Progress Action Fund (www.americanprogressaction.org).

Now, only about 12 percent of the workforce is represented by unions. The middle class's share of the nation's income declined right along with the decline in union membership, down to 46 percent.

Even Ben Bernanke, chairman of the Federal Reserve, who never saw a failing bank he didn't give a free loan to,[4] agrees that unions have an effect on overall wealth distribution. In a 2007 speech, speaking in his professional economist's convoluted way, he said, "Whatever the precise mechanism through which lower rates of unionization affected the wage structure, the available research suggests that it can explain between 10 percent and 20 percent of the rise in wage inequality among men during the 1970s and 1980s."[5] Translation: fewer union members, fewer dollars in your pocket.

It used to be a given that as a worker's productivity increased, the worker's pay went up along with it. If someone earned ten dollars an hour turning out a hundred dollars' worth of widgets, and a few years later he or she was able to turn out two hundred dollars' worth of widgets in the same amount of time, they would expect that their hourly wage would move toward the twenty-dollar range.

Indeed, that's exactly what happened for quite a long time.

Since World War II, worker productivity has increased at an average rate of 2.2 percent a year. Until the 1970s, wages rose along with it. Produce more, earn more—we're all in this together.

In the 1970s, the two trends began to separate. Productivity kept going up, but workers stopped getting their fair share. Starting in the 1980s, the separation grew more extreme. Union membership in the private sector started a slow decline in the late 1950s. That trend accelerated rapidly from the 1980s on.

At the same time membership in public service unions began to rise. In 2011, 37 percent of public service workers belonged to a union. Naturally, as the public sector unionized, the income of public employees went up.

When these two groups are lumped together, the loss of the relationship between income and productivity is partially

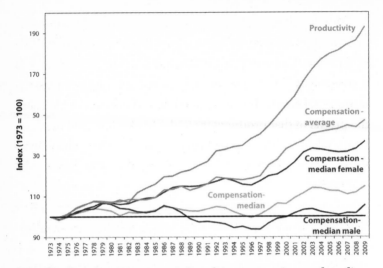

Growth of productivity, average hourly compensation, and median hourly compensation by gender, 1973–2009

Source: Economic Policy Institute, *The State of Working America.* Washington, D.C.: Economic Policy Institute, 2011. www.stateof workingamerica.org/jobs/figure12.

masked. If we strip out public service workers and people in fields like nursing, and look at the manufacturing sector alone, we see how dramatic that disconnection is.

"If American workers were rewarded for 100 percent of their increases in labor productivity between 1980 and 2009—as they were during the middle part of the 20th century—then median wages would be $31.98 per hour, or 61 percent higher than the average real wage in 2009."[6]

Median annual income for full-time workers, ages twenty-five to sixty-four, is about $44,000 a year. A 60 percent increase would take that up to $70,400 a year.

When unions grow weak, workers get less. Even more significant, they stop participating in increased profitability. The difference, the excess profit, started moving upward to top management. There was also a dramatic increase in financialization—takeovers, buyouts, mergers, and the like—which sent the profits of that productivity to the banks, financial manipulators, takeover barons, and big law firms. By 2000, virtually all the increases in profitability were going to the top or to financial maneuvering.

If we continue to let unions decline, Main Street's share of the national income will continue to decline. If union membership goes up, the middle class's share of the national income will go up. If you are anywhere except in the top 1 percent, your income will likely go up.

We were always told that in America, the harder you work the more successful you'll be. The facts show that's not the case anymore. It's time we make it the case again.

Conventional wisdom also says that the rungs on the ladder to higher income are constructed out of diplomas: high school, associate's degree, BA or BS, then a graduate degree. That implicitly makes the claim that high earners have earned their status through discipline, foresight, and hard work, while the income level of low earners, or no earners, is their own darn fault. They should've done their homework instead of skipping class and playing video games.

It is also taken to mean that the only real way for a normal, average person—not a pro athlete, rapper, supermodel, supergenius programmer—to make a better living is to get more schooling. Fighting for better wages, asking for a fair share of your productivity, putting labor ahead of big banks, changes in tax policy, and joining a union as ways to increase your well-being are not even subjects worth discussing.

But that's not true.

According to a study by Bruce Western of Harvard University and Jake Rosenfeld of the University of Washington, Seattle, "Unions, Norms and the Rise of American Earnings Inequality," "Union decline explains one third of the growth in inequality—an effect equal to the growing stratification of earnings by education."[7]

In terms of how much money you personally make, returning union strength to where it was in the 1970s could be as good for you as going to Harvard.

As we endeavor to give everyone a college education, we must eventually pass the point where the number of college graduates exceeds the number of education-worthy jobs. Then we have a peculiar problem: a conundrum where higher education doesn't guarantee stable employment.

Indeed, we have entered that territory.

"For the first time in record keeping history, the unemployment rate for those with 4-year degrees or higher has passed the 4 percent mark."[8]

Last fall, the *New York Times* did a story called "Generation Limbo: Waiting It Out":

"We did everything we were supposed to," said Stephanie Morales, 23, who graduated from Dartmouth College in 2009 with hopes of working in the arts. Instead she ended up waiting tables at a Chart House restaurant in Weehawken, N.J., earning $2.17 an hour plus tips, to pay off her student loans. "What was the point of working so hard for 22 years if there was nothing out there?" said Ms. Morales, who is now a paralegal and plans on attending law school.

Some of Ms. Morales's classmates have found themselves on welfare. "You don't expect someone who just spent four years in Ivy League schools to be on food stamps," said Ms. Morales, who estimates that a half-dozen of her friends are on the Supplemental Nutrition Assistance Program. A few are even helping younger graduates figure out how to apply. "We are passing on these traditions on how to work in the adult world as working poor," Ms. Morales said.[9]

ABC News also did a story on recent college graduates:

"I just graduated from the University of Texas at Austin with a degree in corporate communications and concentrations in business and Chinese," wrote one. "I thought I would be set once I graduated. Of course, I was wrong. In order to pay the bills, I'm doing random odd jobs, such as cleaning and helping people pack."

Another told us: "I'm 22 years old with a degree in management from Hofstra University. I've been job hunting since May 2009. I've been making some money baby-sitting, but I don't want to make a career out of babysitting for the rest of my life."

Or this: "I graduated from Northern Michigan University in August '08 with a BS in mathematics. I have applied for nearly 300 jobs and only heard back from a small handful. Got a personal trainer's certificate."

Trudy Steinfeld, who runs the Wasserman Center for Career Development at New York University . . . says there's no shame in cleaning, babysitting, and personal training. "Obviously, you do whatever you have to do to pay the bills."[10]

Education has great value. A literate and numerate workforce is a better workforce. Education can be a road to upward mobility. Still, it is not, and cannot be, the solution for everyone. Nor can it fix the destabilization of the nation that has resulted from our economic inequalities.

Unless you are a hedge fund manager, or work in the top echelon of one of the banks that brought the world to the brink of ruin, or you've inherited so much money that you're bulletproof, you should fight to save the unions. As they go down, Main Street declines. If union membership goes up, your income goes up.

Few understand the importance of strong unions more than our 1.6 million members. They know the impact not just on themselves and their families, but on the citizens they serve each day at work and on the wider economic landscape in America. As the attacks of 2011 unfolded, they would show unfailing grit when corporate-backed politicians targeted that source of economic strength for the working middle class. Didn't matter if it was in snowy Madison, Wisconsin, or simmering Memphis, Tennessee. They were ready to fight back.

In Wisconsin, groundskeeper Laura Peterson slept overnight on a cold stone floor in the Madison statehouse to ensure that she would be heard in the morning by lawmakers who were weighing whether she deserved her collective bargaining rights.

At the University of California in Berkeley, lead gardener Kathryn Lybarger was leading a big fight against selling off services to privateers. "We're very proud of the work we do, serving the university community," she said. "To ensure that public higher education standards are maintained, we organized against any attempts to weaken our union and take away our rights."

In Lansing, Michigan, elevator inspector Rick Price, a self-described "common guy," protested against the governor at rallies after he rammed through legislation installing emergency managers capable of disbanding elected school boards and city councils and revoking collective bargaining agreements.

Across the country in San Jose, California, Elena Backman was a workers' compensation adjuster and a grandmother, but never an activist. Yet when politicians threatened collective bargaining, hard-earned pensions, and public services, she became an outspoken presence at rallies and city council meetings.

Frank Piccioli, a 911 dispatcher in Phoenix, Arizona, has also vowed to "fight back tooth and nail" against politicians who are bent on doing away with workers' rights. "We field about 1.5 million calls a year with less staff and resources," Piccioli points out. "We want to be part of the solution, but we are being demonized by politicians who are turning their backs on the citizens of Arizona and hurting the very people who save lives."

Dolores Bressette recently retired after thirty-seven years of service to the people of Rhode Island and contributed on time, every time to her own pension. She planned for her pension to provide her security in retirement. Then politicians in Rhode Island took an ax to it. "On the news, I saw them celebrating. It's upsetting that they could do this to us. They don't see us as people. They see us as a number."

In New York City, Lenny Allen fought the state's decision to lay off a thousand workers and revoke another eight hundred retirees' health insurance and supplemental benefits, all while cancer sapped his strength. Further south, in Memphis, Tennessee, sanitation worker Cynthia Hart balanced a grueling schedule at the garbage dumps with an effort to organize her coworkers against the city's plan to privatize their work.

Robert Montuori, a New Haven, Connecticut, custodian, led a similar struggle against privatization attempts by the local school board. "We prevailed because we're determined to preserve the rights and benefits we've fought so hard to gain. If we don't stand together as one, we'll be pulled apart piece by piece. We should never forget how we got to be where we are today."

Across the country, people outraged by these attacks on the American Dream, and tired of seeing jobs lost in their communities, knew that they were up against powerful political and corporate forces. They knew it was going to take a full-fledged movement to win.

CHAPTER THREE

Class Warfare

IF UNIONS ARE SO DARN GREAT—with members, other workers and entire states benefiting—then how come we see the American Dream keep slipping away from the nation's working middle class and an increasing share of wealth being hoarded by those at the top of the income scale?

Because we're in a class war.

You don't have to take our word for it. Here's Warren Buffett, the Oracle of Omaha, one of the world's five wealthiest people: "There's class warfare, all right, but it's my class, the rich class, that's making war, and we're winning."[1]

Mostly you hear the term "class warfare" from only one side of the political spectrum. It's a form of name calling to get away from discussing things on their merits. For example, if someone suggests that we need more regulation of Wall Street, a proposition that is both self-evidently true and supported in great detail by the "Final Report of the National Commission on the Causes of the Financial and Economic Crisis in the United States," the blowhards on Fox News will shriek, "Eek! Class warfare!" If anyone suggests letting the Bush tax cuts for the richest Americans expire because we can't afford them—"Class warfare!" If we point out that Mitt Romney only paid a 13.9 percent tax rate on the income from his vast fortune—far lower than the rest of us—he will say it's all "about envy. It's about class warfare!"[2] (And then he'll try to change the subject by saying his finances aren't handled by him, but by his "trustee"—another luxury, along with that 13.9 percent tax rate, that is completely foreign to most Americans.) And according to Ron Paul, Medicare, Medicaid, and Social Security are class warfare taking us down the road toward dictatorship.[3]

Fairness & Accuracy in Reporting (FAIR) did a study of how the term "class warfare" is used in the media. They looked at four outlets over a nine-month period from November 2008 to April 2009: the *New York Times* and CNN, who regard themselves as politically neutral practitioners of objective journalism, and Fox News and the *Washington Times*, both openly owned and operated house organs of the political right.

The study found "a striking bias." "Class warfare" and related terms were used, almost exclusively, against efforts to improve conditions on Main Street or to restrict the excesses of Wall Street. It was almost never used to describe programs that ripped off ordinary people or that allowed the super greedy to gorge on more gold.

"The bias held across the outlets, but fell into two distinct groups: significantly unbalanced and completely unbalanced. At the *New York Times*, descriptions of 'class warfare' as bottom-up outnumbered top-down descriptions 6-to-1, while at CNN the imbalance was 8-to-1.

"The right-wing outlets in our sample, Fox and the *Washington Times*, never presented 'class warfare' as anything other than action taken on behalf of the poor or against the wealthy."[4]

As FAIR describes it, "Bottom-up 'class warfare' references suggest that lower economic classes are openly hostile and irrational, seeking the destruction of the rich even to the ruin of the nation."[5] Class war references continue to be used primarily by the right. The horde of contenders in 2011–2012 to be the Republican nominee for president all used it routinely in reference to President Obama.

Joe Klein, in an October 2011 *Time* article called "Class Warfare: The Middle Class Is Losing," wrote: "Newt Gingrich inimitably put it to a crowd in Davenport, Iowa . . . 'The President is a sincere believer in class warfare radicalism.'"

Reverend Jim Wallis, the head of Sojourners, an organization that believes Jesus Christ taught the principles of social justice and helping the poor, said, "So why is it when the top 1 percent of the country controls 42 percent of the nation's financial wealth—more than 90 percent of the rest of us—and the ratio of CEO pay to average workers' salaries is 400 to 1, it is *not* class warfare? Yet simply calling for a return of the highest-end tax rates to the 1990s levels *is*?"[6]

Let's be very clear: this is not an argument about capitalism versus communism, or the free market versus socialism. Class warfare, as it is really practiced in America, is about the top 1 percent grabbing a dominant share of all of our nation's income and all of our wealth.

There are certainly moral reasons, deeply rooted in American values, to argue against excessive income inequality. If people work harder and increase their productivity, it's only fair that they share in the increase in profits. But as we saw earlier, that no longer happens.

The last time we had the degree of inequality that we have now, the year was 1928. What followed was the crash of 1929 and the Great Depression. That was followed by the New Deal, which included higher taxes on the rich, financial regulations, government investment in infrastructure through the Work Projects Administration (WPA) and education through the GI Bill, the National Labor Relations Act, the ability for everyone to participate in earned-benefit programs like Social Security, unemployment insurance, workers' compensation, and later on, Medicare.

In short, the New Deal leveled the playing field so that everyone had a shot at the American Dream. The period that ensued, roughly 1940 to 1980, is now referred to as the Great Compression.[7]

The Great Compression was a period of unprecedented growth and stability. Howard M. Wachtel, in *Street of Dreams—Boulevard of Broken Hearts: Wall Street's First Century,* wrote that "the regulatory regime established during the 1930s prevailed until its undoing in the deregulatory movement of the 1980s. In that half-century the American economy grew faster than in any other comparable period in history. It was also the only such half-century without a single or even minor financial crisis on Wall Street, which had become used to one every ten years or so from its origins in 1792 to the 1930s."[8]

We have since moved away from this common sense investment that put the American Dream within reach and instead

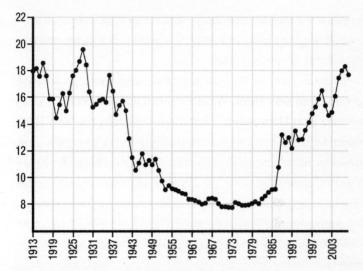

Top 1 percent income shares, United States, 1913–2008

Source: The World Top Incomes Database, http://g-mond.paris schoolofeconomics.eu/topincomes. Piketty & Saez, 2007.

have embraced policies and rhetoric that have nearly killed it. When we finally reached the degree of income inequality that existed in 1929, it happened all over again. This time we got the crash of 2008. Thanks to government intervention, including President Obama's American Recovery and Reinvestment Act of 2009, it did not turn into a true depression. Sadly, and contrary to conventional wisdom in Washington, D.C., the government's investment wasn't big enough and little was done to narrow the gap between rich and poor. So instead of sinking into a depression, the Great Recession lingered on.

The great transfer of wealth from the working middle class to the super rich did not happen by accident. It was the product of planning and investment. In 1971, Lewis F. Powell Jr. wrote an action plan on how to do it. Think of it as a corporate take-over of the American Dream.

Powell was a prominent attorney on his way to becoming a Supreme Court justice. He was on the board of directors of several corporations, most notably the tobacco company Philip Morris. He was very upset about all the disturbing leftist, anti-establishment trends in America. He was particularly crazed by consumer advocates like Ralph Nader who made the outrageous suggestion that corporations should be held to account for their actions.

Bear in mind that Philip Morris sold tobacco, a product that killed people, often in slow, agonizing ways. Philip Morris executives knew it, but tried to hide that knowledge. They commissioned junk science and had it published in order to throw mud and murk onto the public debate. After all, what would happen if people who knowingly conspire to kill other people, even through legal means and hidden behind a corporate veil, were really accountable, even to the point of going to jail like common criminals? Powell couldn't have that.

He wrote up a confidential memorandum for the U.S. Chamber of Commerce with the title "Attack on the Free Enterprise System." Although American companies were the largest in the world, enjoying unprecedented revenues and profits, Powell had become very nervous about how criticism of corporate America was not coming from the extreme left but "from perfectly respectable elements of society: from the college campus, the pulpit, the media, the intellectual and literary journals, the arts and sciences, and from politicians."[9]

There was, Powell argued, a "massive assault upon [business's] fundamental economics."

Oddly, and tellingly, one specific issue raised his ire. "Favorite current targets are proposals for tax incentives through changes in depreciation rates and investment credits. These are usually described in the media as 'tax breaks,' 'loop holes' or 'tax benefits' for the benefit of business. As viewed by a columnist in the *Post*, such tax measures would benefit 'only the rich, the owners of big companies.'"

To Powell's way of thinking, even describing tax breaks as "tax breaks" was disturbing and had to be stopped.

Powell was very disturbed that businesses had taken these assaults lying down. The memorandum called for a counter-attack.

The Chamber of Commerce would be the command and control center. The politburo of the corporate counter-revolution. "Independent and uncoordinated activity by individual corporations, as important as this is, will not be sufficient. Strength lies in organization, in careful long-range planning and implementation, in consistency of action over an indefinite period of years, in the scale of financing available only through joint effort, and in the political power available only through united action and national organizations."

Powell then selected key targets and described the tactics.

The first thing to do was to go after intellectual centers, university campuses, by setting up a counter-intelligentsia. A "Staff of Scholars" needed to be recruited who could develop the profit-at-all-cost message. They would overlap with a "Staff of Speakers," who would deliver the gospel of gold. There would be a "Speaker's Bureau" to get them booked into significant venues, and, obviously, get them fees. With that set up the "Chamber should insist upon equal time on the college speaking circuit."

Powell acknowledged that it was not likely that anyone would want to hear such speakers. In a true free market of ideas they'd never get booked "unless the Chamber aggressively insisted upon the right to be heard—in effect, insisted upon 'equal time,' . . . and exert[ed] whatever degree of pressure—publicly and privately—may be necessary to assure opportunities to speak."

These sponsored scholars needed to publish in scholarly journals, just like real scholars, and there should be "incentives" to encourage them to do so. In addition, they should send out their articles to popular magazines.

They should insist on "Balancing of Faculties," demanding university jobs for conservatives, though it would be "indeed a long-range and difficult project."

There should also be "Evaluation of Textbooks" to ensure that they become more fair to the free enterprise system or, as Fox News phrases it, "fair and balanced."

Once they got the universities, the memo said, they should go after secondary education.

They would try to influence the general public in the same way: "establish the staffs of eminent scholars, writers and speakers, who will do the thinking, the analysis, the writing and the speaking. It will also be essential to have staff personnel who are thoroughly familiar with the media, and how most effectively to communicate with the public. . . .

"The national television networks should be monitored in the same way that textbooks should be kept under constant surveillance." Anytime anyone said anything critical of business they would have to be challenged. Followed by a demand for equal time and threats to go to the FCC. The same should be done with radio and print media.

The chamber should be used for lobbying. If a corporation wanted something the public hated, and was afraid it would lead to consumer boycotts or even criticism, they could funnel the money to the Chamber of Commerce in order to lobby for policy without being associated with the policy. Also, there were many issues that would benefit many businesses, so it would be more effective to bundle their efforts.

Powell wrote that "under our constitutional system, especially with an activist-minded Supreme Court, the judiciary may be the most important instrument for social, economic and political change." Therefore corporations needed to go after the legal system, and especially appear as *amici curiae*, so that they could appear in front of judges, especially the justices of the Supreme Court.

Corporations should mobilize their stockholders. Every major corporation should have a public relations staff associated with the program.

Joseph Coors, the beer tycoon, was "stirred" by the memo.[10] He founded the Heritage Foundation in 1973 as a home for the sort of scholars that Powell dreamed of, where they remain, to this very day, happily churning out puffery for corporate interests. James Olin was influenced by the Powell memo as well.[11] His Olin Foundation was a heavy contributor to all the right-wing propaganda mills, including the American Enterprise Institute (AEI), the Heritage Foundation, the Hoover Institution on War, Revolution and Peace, the Hudson Institute, and the Project for the New American Century (PNAC).

The Chamber of Commerce is now the organization that Powell dreamed of, receiving huge sums from corporate interests, keeping their donors and their spending secret, to influence politics. According to a *New York Times* report, Prudential Financial donated $2 million in 2009 to the Chamber of Commerce, just as it was beginning a national advertising campaign "to weaken the historic rewrite of the nation's financial regulations."[12] That same year Dow Chemical donated $1.7 million to the chamber as it "took a leading role in aggressively fighting proposed rules that would impose tighter security requirements on chemical facilities."

The report continued, "And Goldman Sachs, Chevron Texaco, and Aegon, a multinational insurance company based in the Netherlands, donated more than $8 million in recent years to a chamber foundation that has been critical of growing federal regulation and spending. These large donations—none of which were publicly disclosed by the chamber, a tax-exempt group that keeps its donors secret, as it is allowed by law—offer a glimpse of the chamber's money-raising efforts . . . health insurance providers funneled at least $10 million to the chamber last year, all of it anonymously, to oppose President Obama's health care legislation."

The *New York Times* noted that the chamber's overall budget had ballooned over the last decade from $130 million in 2003 to $200 million. In 2009 alone the chamber and its affiliates spent $144 million for lobbying, making it the biggest lobbyist in the United States.

As for Powell himself, Richard Nixon nominated him to the Supreme Court. So he kept the memo secret. It wouldn't look good if the public knew that a future Supreme Court justice was plotting a corporate takeover of the American Dream.

CHAPTER FOUR

Class Warriors:
The Koch Brothers and ALEC

THE KOCH BROTHERS, David and Charles, are billionaires who head up Koch Industries and have certainly found a niche for themselves in Lewis Powell's movement. They earned their money the old-fashioned way. They were born into it. To be fair, "the company has grown spectacularly since their father, Fred, died, in 1967, and the brothers took charge."[1] The Koch brothers are the new epicenter of the pro-corporate network that Powell dreamed of.

It's not the sort of network you find in an action thriller like *The Bourne Identity*. It's looser and much less formal. A single heroic agent, even with stunt doubles, can hardly put an end to it. Nor will it die with exposure to the light of day. Its roots are much deeper and its reach is much broader.

David Koch used to joke that Koch Industries was "the biggest company you've never heard of."[2] According to *Forbes* magazine, it's the second-largest privately owned company in America, so you can't buy or sell shares of Koch Industries on the stock market. *Forbes* estimates its revenues at $100 billion a year.[3] It's a conglomerate that's in oil, pipelines, refining, chemicals, polymers, fibers, fertilizers, minerals, bulk transporting, ranching, commodity trading, timber, and paper.[4] The products best known to the public come from its subsidiary, Georgia-Pacific, which makes Brawny, Coronet, Quilted Northern, and Dixie cups. Another of their companies, Invista, makes Lycra, Dacron, Stainmaster, and Polarguard.

David and Charles Koch have an ideology as radical as Marxism. They, too, want to make government wither away and die. But when it's gone, they want corporate rule, rather than a workers' paradise, to spring forth. Every little step closer to their goal enriches the brothers personally. Fewer environmental rules, less enforcement, no Justice Department to go after them for price fixing or stealing from public lands, harder for people they hurt to go to court, and limits on damages are all things that make the Koch brothers happier and wealthier.

But they are also true believers in this ideology. In an interview, David Koch once said, "It's something I grew up with—a fundamental point of view that big government was bad, and imposition of government controls on our lives and economic fortunes was not good."[5]

In June 2011, the Kochs hosted a seminar at the Ritz-Carlton Bachelor Gulch Hotel in Avon, Colorado, at the foot of Beaver Creek Mountain.

According to kochfacts.com, a PR website sponsored by Koch Industries, these seminars are benign affairs "that bring together some of America's greatest philanthropists and most successful business leaders whose companies have created millions of jobs. Attendees discuss solutions to our most pressing issues and strategies to promote policies that will help grow our economy, foster free enterprise and create American jobs."[6]

Yet they go to great lengths to keep them secret. "Audio technicians even set up outward-pointing speakers around the perimeter of the outdoor dining pavilion, according to sources, emitting static to frustrate would-be eavesdroppers."[7]

The *New York Times* got hold of a secret invitation to a January 2011 seminar. "The Kochs insist on strict confidentiality."[8] The letter advises participants that it is closed to the public, including the news media, and admonishes them not to post updates or information about the meeting on the Web, blogs, social media, or traditional media, and to "be mindful of the security and confidentiality of your meeting notes and materials."[9]

These "seminars" have been going for a long time. Hundreds of people attend each one. Participants have included Rush Limbaugh, Glenn Beck, Senator Jim DeMint (R-SC), Senator Tom Coburn (R-OK), Representative Paul Ryan (R-WI), Representative Mike Pence (R-IN), Florida Governor Rick Scott, Virginia Governor Robert McDonnell, Texas Governor Rick Perry, and Supreme Court justices Antonin Scalia and Clarence Thomas. In spite of that they have managed to fly under the radar, only coming to public notice in 2010.

In 2011, someone smuggled a recording device into the Colorado event and brought out a tape of Charles Koch addressing the crowd. Intent on rousing them to give and then give more to beat Obama in 2012, he said, "We have Saddam

Hussein, this is the Mother of All Wars we've got in the next 18 months. For the life or death of this country."[10] Then he went on to thank people who had put up money for the cause. "What I want to do is recognize not all of our great partners, but those partners who have given more than . . . a million over the last 12 months." He listed thirty-three of them. Thirty-three sets of deep pockets who had put up more than a million dollars each, in the previous year, for the Koch brothers' select political causes.

It is impossible to know how much they themselves spend. The money that we do know about, that appears on the record, is delivered from more tentacles than reach out from an octopus. As Jane Mayer reported in the *New Yorker*:

> Since 1998 Koch Industries has spent more than fifty million dollars on lobbying. Separately, the company's political-action committee, KochPAC, has donated some eight million dollars to political campaigns, more than eighty percent of it to Republicans. So far in 2010, Koch Industries leads all other energy companies in political contributions, as it has since 2006. In addition, during the past dozen years the Kochs and other family members have personally spent more than two million dollars on political contributions. In the second quarter of 2010, David Koch was the biggest individual contributor to the Republican Governors Association, with a million-dollar donation. Other gifts by the Kochs may be untraceable; federal tax law permits anonymous personal donations to politically active nonprofit groups.[11]

The effort runs long and deep. Back in 1977, they funded the Cato Institute. A decade later they contributed millions toward the Mercatus Center at George Mason University. It was described by the *Wall Street Journal* as "the most important think tank you've never heard of."[12]

The Koch brothers also have a wide variety of front groups like Americans for Prosperity, FreedomWorks, and Citizens for a Sound Economy.

"Americans for Prosperity pledged to spend $45 million on rallies, canvassing and hard-hitting radio and television ads criticizing Democrats in 50 swing House districts and half a dozen targeted Senate races"[13] for the 2010 midterm elections.

One of the institutions that they bankroll is the blandly named American Legislative Exchange Council (ALEC). ALEC has been, until recently, a very obscure organization. The masthead of its website reads "limited government · free markets · federalism." The mission statement speaks about Jeffersonian principals and claims to be nonpartisan. If partisanship is defined strictly as party affiliation, it is marginally true. If partisanship means adherence to corporatist principals and enlisting as one of the troopers on the side of wealth against the rights of Main Street, then it is very partisan indeed. ALEC holds behind-closed-door meetings between pro-corporate politicians and corporate lobbyists, all underwritten by powerful special interests, including the insurance and banking industries, big oil, and the pharmaceutical giants.

Per ALECwatch.org, big corporations lay out more than $6 million a year to wine and dine state legislators, and pay for expensive vacations and junkets, while at the same time drafting corporate-friendly legislation that the politicians then push when they return to their statehouses. This covert coalition of state legislators and Wall Street moneymen has been surreptitiously working out of the view of Main Street Americans to dismantle health, safety, and environmental regulations, privatize vital public services, restrict the ability of working men and women to make a fair wage, and reduce the ability of seniors, students, minorities, and the poor to vote. All done without the press or public seeing whose palm is greased.

(Florida state Representative Rachel Burgin may have missed ALEC's memo about being covert. In February 2012, Burgin introduced legislation calling on the federal government to reduce corporate taxes. One problem: she forgot to remove the ALEC mission statement the group puts in as a placeholder to be deleted in model legislation it writes for lawmakers.)

More than two thousand state legislators like Burgin are in on the game. Over the years, with corporate backing in their campaigns, they often go for higher office, like former ALEC members in Congress, Speaker of the House John Boehner and House Majority Leader Eric Cantor. More than seventy members of Congress and governors have attended the closed-to-the public get-togethers where corporate CEOs lay out the agenda for the year ahead.

How does ALEC work? Here's an explanation from Tommy Thompson, four-term Republican governor of Wisconsin (1987–2001) and secretary of Health and Human Services under President George W. Bush. In a speech at ALEC's 2002 annual meeting he "fondly remembers his days as a state rep and an early ALEC member in the 1970s. 'Myself, I always loved going to these meetings because I always found new ideas. Then I'd take them back to Wisconsin, disguise them a little bit, and declare that "It's mine."""[14]

A 2010 report by the American Association for Justice describes how ALEC advances the interests of powerful corporations against working families across the country. "ALEC's campaigns and model legislation have run the gamut of issues," they concluded, "but all have either protected or promoted a corporate revenue stream, often at the expense of consumers."[15]

ALEC has worked on behalf of telecom firms to block low-cost municipally owned broadband. They've pushed bills, backed by the big banks, to force seniors to take out reverse mortgages before they can receive Medicaid. They've restricted the ability of states to require insurers to meet strengthened accounting and auditing rules. Tobacco companies draft laws to limit lawsuits targeting their deadly products, while the private prison industry uses its clout in ALEC to push state laws, like Arizona's anti-immigration legislation, to provide a steady stream of undocumented workers that it can jail in its detention centers.

The Wall Street barons take a tax deduction for the money they contribute to their secret cabal. Publicly traded companies such as tobacco giant Altria (previously Philip Morris) and well-known corporations such as AT&T, Boeing, ExxonMobil, and Coca-Cola are all contributing big bucks, using company funds to undermine the legislative process.

They cynically form committees to write "model laws" hand in hand with compliant legislators, all while enjoying golf outings and lavish dinners far from the view of the public and press. Common Cause, the organization that champions good government, has called on the IRS to investigate, noting that

ALEC's influence peddling "does an end-run around state ethics laws intended to restrict the ability of businesses to buy access to legislators in order to promote their policy agendas."[16] ALEC is little more than a shadowy influence-peddling operation disguised as a public charity.

Justice Louis Brandeis called state legislatures "the laboratories of democracy," highlighting their ability to find innovative alternatives in the way each state would be governed. Today, however, the insidious ALEC turns state legislatures into laboratories of deceit, where laws are presented for consideration after being crafted in secret meetings by some of the largest international corporations. The powerful interests participating in this covert council are pushing their agenda away from the view of the public, the press, and without the accountability that Americans expect from those who write our laws.

These efforts fly in the face of basic American values. This hidden collusion between well-financed lobbyists and elected legislators undermines public debate and full-disclosure that Americans rightly expect when our laws are made.

Before the New Deal, class warfare by the rich against working people was fought in much more naked and violent ways.

In 1931, coal miners went on strike in Harlan County, Kentucky.

The miners lived in shacks owned by the companies. They didn't get paid in money. They got paid in scrip. The scrip could only be spent at the company store, where things cost 50 to 100 percent more than in real stores. It cost a miner more to live than he could possibly earn. (*"Saint Peter don't you call me / 'cause I can't go / I owe my soul to the company store."*[17]) The owners kept newspapers out of their towns and they read the miners' mail. The owners called miners who wanted a union communists, they called them radicals, they called them Reds. The companies had spies. As soon as a man joined the union he was blacklisted, evicted from his company home, and cut off at the company store. The mine owners owned every politician, judge, and lawman in the county. The *Knoxville News-Sentinel* wrote: "It seemed like the old feudal system argument that the slave can have nothing to say as to his master's treatment of him."[18]

The conflict would go on for nine years. In the middle of it, in 1935, the governor named a commission to investigate. Their report said: "There exists a virtual reign of terror [in Harlan County], financed in general by a group of coal mine operators in collusion with certain public officials: the victims of this reign of terror are the coal miners and their families."[19]

The chief enforcer was Sheriff, J. H. Blair. "I did all in my power to aid the coal operators."[20] He had 170 deputies. One hundred and sixty-four of them were on coal company payrolls. Blair told a reporter, "Hell, yes, I've issued orders to shoot to kill."[21]

The sheriff and his men entered the home of Florence Reese, looking for her husband, a union organizer. They tried to terrorize her and her children. When they finally left, she took a calendar down off the wall, and to the tune of an old hymn, she wrote a song, "Which Side Are You On?"

The lyrics went, "*They say in Harlan County, there are no neutrals there. You either are a union man, or a thug for J. H. Blair.*"

We're all sitting here, in relative safety and security. We don't think Sheriff Blair is going to kick the door in. We think that's just the bad old days. Things are not so desperate.

We may owe several thousands of dollars on credit cards to Citigroup, Bank of America, and the like, at 14.56 percent interest.[22] We're proud of our children for graduating college. Should we be upset that they're getting started in real life with a college loan debt of $25,000?[23] Also, there's the fact that the unemployment rate for new college grads is over 9 percent. We watched the government bail out the banks to the tune of $700 billion. Yet there's no money for jobs, small businesses, public works projects, rebuilding our infrastructure. CEOs, even those who drove their companies to bankruptcy, make more and more, while our biggest retailers, our fast food chains, and a host of other businesses pay wages so low that some portion of their employees are on public assistance for medical care and for food.

Still, it's not the bad old days.

Yet.

In class warfare, the top class—call them the major corporations, the super rich, the big banks, the organizations they fund—will do whatever they can. Some of them will always go at least two yards over the limit of what everyone thinks they can get away with. If they do get away with it, that becomes the new borderline. If other companies in the same business want to stay competitive, they have to. If no one stops them, the boundaries keep moving outward.

And unless you're in the top 1 percent, and you're making $500,000 a year or more, that war is against you. Obviously, there are lots of people who make less than that who think the Tea Party is where the answers are, or who want to coddle and support too-big-to-fail banks, and think that multinational corporations are frail creatures that need all the help they can get from American voters and taxpayers. If that's how you feel, we'd like to suggest that you're making a mistake and we'd ask you to reconsider.

If someone is waging war on us and we don't even acknowledge that it's taking place, they will win and we will lose. Let's not be afraid of the words. There's a class war going on. They started it. They're winning. It's time to fight back.

CHAPTER FIVE

General Electric

A T FIRST WE THOUGHT we would include this in the chapter about class warfare. But then we thought this single, stunning fact tells you everything you need to know about why things are so out of whack with the American Dream today. So we decided to let it stand on its own.

In 2011, the U.S. House of Representatives, blaming budget shortfalls, voted to slash hundreds of billions of dollars from Social Security, Medicare, and Medicaid. The year before, thanks to corporate tax loopholes and other perfectly legal tax tricks, General Electric, one of the largest corporations in the world, did not pay a dime in federal income tax despite posting a $5.1 billion profit in the United States.

Enough said.

CHAPTER SIX

The Last Line of Defense

IF WE GRANT that there is class warfare, or at least that businesses often prefer not to have unions, that still doesn't explain the decline of union membership.

Nor why John Kasich is going after BJ Simmons-Talley and blaming her for all of Ohio's woes.

The media myth of the decline of unions makes it sound as if it's the result of natural forces. An inevitable form of evolution like the disappearance of the dodo. As third-world countries became emerging nations, they learned modern technologies. With low wages, few safety and health rules, and little in the way of environmental regulations, they can produce manufactured goods at a far lower cost than we can.

That made our industrial wage rates uncompetitive. Those old-fashioned union contracts put health and pension obligations on our great industrial companies that were too heavy to bear, and that was part of our decline as a manufacturing nation.

Yes, once upon a time, the story goes, there was a genuine need for unions. You know, back in the bad old days—like in Harlan County, when miners could only shop at the company store, their families wore rags and went hungry, while goons with pistols and clubs enforced the company's rules—maybe then unions served a purpose.

But according to myth, in our modern workplaces, with profit sharing, stock options, flex work, bosses in jeans, and trendy trends, there's no need for organized labor.

The rise and fall of unions in America does not correlate with economic conditions. It does not correlate with the nature of the economy. It does not correlate with international competition or the nature of the workplace.

There's been plenty of passion and courage, drama and violence in American labor history. The Great Railroad Strike of 1877 saw pitched battles in West Virginia, Maryland, Pennsylvania, Illinois, and Missouri. Local law enforcement, the militias, vigilantes, and the National Guard put together couldn't break the workers. Finally, President Rutherford B. Hayes had to dispatch federal troops, moving from city to city, like it was a military campaign of conquest.

The next two decades were marked by a massive upsurge in strike action and employee violence. In 1886 in Milwaukee, seven people were killed when the governor ordered the state militia to shoot into a crowd of demonstrating workers. In 1892, the Pinkertons—the Blackwater military contractors of their day, providing armed enforcers for anyone who could pay—went to war against the steelworkers in Homestead, Pennsylvania. Seven guards and eleven strikers died in the shootout. Labor activists were hanged in the coalfields, charged with being members of the Molly Maguires, an organization of anti-landlord terrorists from back in Ireland. It took federal troops to end the Pullman Strike of 1894.

In 1904, the Colorado Militia battled strikers. They killed six, took fifteen of them prisoner, and deported seventy-nine to Kansas. The year 1912 saw militias called in West Virginia against the coal miners and in Louisiana against the timber workers. In 1914, company thugs hired by John D. Rockefeller opened fire with machine guns on union families in Ludlow, Colorado, who were camped out in tents, killing five men, two women, and twelve children. In 1917, an organizer for the Industrial Workers of the World, the Wobblies, was lynched in Butte, Montana. Federal agents, meanwhile, raided Industrial Workers of the World offices in forty-eight cities. In the 1920s the offices of the National Textile Workers Union were demolished by a hundred masked men. In 1930, one hundred farm workers were arrested for trying to organize. In 1932, Dearborn, Michigan, police and security guards working for the Ford Motor Company fired on marching workers, killing five and injuring sixty. Twenty-five Dearborn police were injured by thrown rocks.

All that strife, and all that blood, had only a marginal effect on union membership.

What happened in 1935 that allowed union membership to shoot up suddenly?

Government. The Franklin D. Roosevelt administration decided that workers had rights and that government should stand up for them.

To be clear, government is not the only reason more workers joined unions. But for the purposes of this book, and

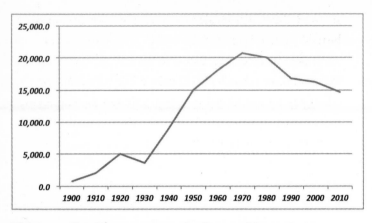

Union membership, 1900–2011 (in thousands)

Source: © 2012 by Barry T. Hirsch and David A. Macpherson.

because we happen to be the elected leaders of a public service union, we will focus on its impact. The National Labor Relations Act, usually called the Wagner Act, was passed in 1935, making it illegal for companies to engage in their standard union-busting tactics. They could not stop employees from trying to organize. Once there was a union, an employer was required to enter into collective bargaining with it. It set up the National Labor Relations Board (NLRB) to enforce the law. It said that an employee could not be fired, or even sent to sit in the basement beneath a water leak, for filing charges with or testifying to the NLRB.

That was followed by the Byrnes Act of 1936, which "made it a felony to transport any person in interstate commerce who was employed for the purpose of using force of threats against non-violent picketing in a labor dispute or against organizing or bargaining efforts. . . ."

In 1936, the Walsh-Healey Act stated that workers must be paid not less than the "prevailing minimum wage" normally paid in a locality; restricted regular working hours to eight hours a day and 40 hours a week, with time-and-a-half pay for additional hours; prohibited the employment of convicts and children under 18; and established sanitation and safety standards.[1]

In 1938 the Fair Labor Standards Act "established minimum wages and maximum hours for all workers engaged in covered 'interstate commerce.'"[2]

The Harlan County coal miners' strike of 1931 was suppressed, but it didn't really end. It continued through the entire decade. In 1935 "the reform-minded county attorney Elmon Middleton was killed when a huge car bomb destroyed his automobile, sending a part of the engine a quarter mile away."[3] Pressure from the federal government let the United Mine Workers back in to attempt to organize. But it didn't keep them safe. "Bombs destroyed two union organizers' cars in January 1937, and that same month snipers shot at a union leader and his wife as they were out walking. On February 9, 1937, three cars drove up in front of that organizer's home and fired a barrage of some twenty-five shots into the house. His wife and a son were slightly wounded. Another son, an innocent teenage boy, was killed."[4] But organize they did. In April 1939, the miners struck against every mine in the county. The governor sent in the National Guard on the side of the operators to force open the mines.

On July 12, guardsmen opened fire on unarmed picketers. They killed two and wounded three. War was about to break out again in Harlan County.

Then the federal government stepped in and forced the companies to settle with the unions.

American workers succeeded when the government got off the sidelines, where it has spent the bulk of its time, and leveled the playing field to make it possible for them to organize.

In 1947, Congress passed the Taft-Hartley Act, a mean-spirited law intended to reverse many of the gains that trade unions and working people had won since the New Deal. President Harry Truman vetoed it. He said:

> I vetoed this bill because I am convinced it is a bad bill. It is bad for labor, bad for management, and bad for the country. . . .
>
> The bill is deliberately designed to weaken labor unions. When the sponsors of the bill claim that by weakening unions, they are giving rights back to individual workingmen, they ignore the basic reason why unions are important in our democracy. Unions exist so that laboring men can bargain with their employers on a basis of equality. Because of unions, the living standards of our working people have increased steadily until they are today the highest in the world. . . .
>
> The Taft-Hartley bill would . . . take us back in the direction of the old evils of individual bargaining. It would take the bargaining power away from the workers and give more power to management. . . .

This bill would again expose workers to the abuses of labor injunctions. . . .

It would make unions liable for damage suits for actions which have long been considered lawful. . . .

The bill would soon upset security clauses in thousands of existing agreements between labor and a number of its provisions deprive workers of legal protection of fundamental rights. They would then have no means of protecting these rights except by striking. . . .

The bill would open up opportunities for endless law suits by employers against unions . . .

. . . it would threaten fundamental democratic freedoms. One provision undertakes to prevent political contributions and expenditures by labor organizations and corporations. This provision would forbid a union newspaper from commenting on candidates in national elections. . . .

I regard this provision of the Taft-Hartley bill as a dangerous challenge to free speech and our free press.

For the sake of the future of this Nation, I hope that this bill will not become law.[5]

Congress passed Taft-Hartley over the president's veto. In addition to the items mentioned in the president's statement, it took away the right to have political strikes and solidarity strikes. It forbade mass picketing. It forbade secondary picketing. It made supervisors part of management, outside of union jurisdiction, and they could be fired for supporting unions. It allowed states to outlaw even those types of union shops with so-called right-to-work laws.

At that point, the growth in union membership began to slow down.

President Ronald Reagan is famous for delivering the next major blow against unions. In 1981, the Professional Air Traffic Controllers Organization (PATCO) went on strike. They had backed Reagan in the 1980 election. He made promises in return.

A Reagan Letter to Robert Poli, PATCO
(Oct. 20, 1980)

Dear Mr. Poli:

I have been briefed by members of my staff as
to the deplorable state of our nation's air traffic
control system. They have told me that too few
people working unreasonable hours with
obsolete equipment has placed the nation's
air travellers in unwarranted danger. In an area
so clearly related to public safety the Carter
administration has failed to act responsibly.
   You can rest assured that if I am elected
President, I will take whatever steps are
necessary to provide our air traffic controllers
with the most modern equipment available and
to adjust staff levels and work days so that they
are commensurate with achieving a maximum
degree of public safety. . . .
   I pledge to you that my administration will
work very closely with you to bring about a

spirit of cooperation between the President and
the air traffic controllers.

Sincerely,
Ronald Reagan[6]

Unfortunately, the union trusted him. The president ordered them back to work. The vast majority stayed out and
Reagan fired every single person who honored the strike:
11,345 people. Just to rub it in, he banned them from federal
jobs for life. The union was decertified.

Alan Greenspan, then chairman of the Federal Reserve
whose policies were a contributing cause of income inequality
and the Great Recession, approved. Reagan's "action gave
weight to the legal right of private employers, previously not
fully exercised, to use their own discretion to both hire and dis-
charge workers."[7]

Up until then, it was presumed to be an implicit part of
good-faith collective bargaining that workers would keep their
jobs even though they were on strike, with their pensions, benefits, seniority, and all the rest. After Reagan that was no longer
the case.

Historian Joseph McCartin, who wrote *Collision Course:
Ronald Reagan, the Air Traffic Controllers, and the Strike that
Changed America,* said in an National Public Radio interview,
"Any kind of worker, it seemed, was vulnerable to replacement
if they went out on strike, and the psychological impact of that,
I think, was huge. The loss of the strike as a weapon for Amer-
ican workers has some rather profound, long-range conse-
quences."[8] It effectively took unions' primary weapon away

from them. It made going on strike so dangerous that "major strikes plummeted from an average of 300 each year in the decades before to fewer than 30 today."[9]

Reagan's breaking of the PATCO strike was, as Harold Meyerson of the *American Prospect* argued, "The signal event in the evisceration of the American middle class."[10] Journalist John Judis argued that "Reagan heralded the end of a political era when labor unions—and the workers they represented—were an integral part of the American social contract."[11]

"Until President Reagan's aggressive response to the air traffic controllers, no president had ever fired thousands of striking workers," *New York Times* labor reporter Steven Greenhouse writes in his book, *The Big Squeeze*:

> Neither had a president ever dissolved a union before.... With the union routed, many companies now felt they could borrow from the president's playbook. Traditionally companies that were hit by strikes hired temporary replacement workers, and the strikers knew that once their walkout ended, their employers would bring them back ... but now companies began hiring permanent replacement workers.
>
> Boise Cascade, Greyhound, Eastern Airlines, International Paper—all embraced replacement workers. In strike after strike, the union was voted out or it surrendered.... Seeing the disastrous results of these walkouts, unions and their members increasingly hesitated to use their most powerful weapon: the strike....
>
> The percentage of truck drivers who belonged to unions plunged from 60 percent in 1975 to 25 percent in

2000. . . . Drivers' pay fell 30 percent after factoring in inflation. . . . Telecommunications workers in unions fell from 55 percent in 1983 to 29 percent a quarter century later, with nonunion typically earning 25 percent less than unionized ones.[12]

Private sector unions went into rapid decline.

But in the public sector, there was a completely different story.

In 1960, there were just 1,070,000 people in public service unions.

In 1970, there were 2,318,000 members of public service unions.

By 1993, it was 7 million. Now there are nearly 8 million.

What happened?

Government.

A unionized workforce is a key factor in determining how much everyone makes. In setting standards for retirement security and health care. In determining what kinds of rights become customary in the workplace, even in nonunion workplaces.

Government is a significant factor in how strong that unionized workforce is. Whether the governor sends the National Guard to roust the workers and open the factories. Whether the federal government passes laws that give people the right to organize and then enforces the rules so that workers can actually do so. Whether states will issue executive orders or pass laws that allow public service workers to negotiate safe working conditions.

Up until the late 1950s public employees essentially had no collective bargaining rights. Public employees were forbidden to strike. In 1959, Wisconsin became the first state to allow collective bargaining. In 1962, President John F. Kennedy signed an executive order that allowed federal employees to be represented by labor organizations. Other states began to follow suit, starting with Michigan, New York, Washington, and Pennsylvania.

Wisconsin—under "Fighting Bob" La Follette Sr., first as its governor, then its senator—had been a laboratory of progressivism. In the good government tradition that was a feature of progressivism, he helped propose the Civil Service Reform Act of 1905. In 1911, due to his influence, Wisconsin passed the first workers' compensation law. His son followed in his footsteps. Running as a Republican, Philip La Follette became governor of Wisconsin in 1931. His policies were precursors to what was about to happen nationally as the New Deal.

Under the original Wisconsin constitution, not altered until 1967, the governor served a two-year term. La Follette was defeated in the Republican gubernatorial primary of 1932. President Herbert Hoover, the man who had ushered in the Great Depression, was going to be at the head of the Republican presidential ticket, seeking a second term as president. Everybody expected that the Democrats were going to sweep the nation and Wisconsin with it. "To the victor go the spoils" was the ethos of the period. It was expected that the Democrats, following the classic model, would surely kick out all those good, clean civil servants, and replace them with ward bosses, supporters, and family members. La Follette's people looked for a way to stop them.

In May 1932, a group of state workers met to decide what to do about it. They viewed public service as a noble occupation and didn't think they should be tossed out of a job just because a new governor had been elected. "Within the hour they formed the Wisconsin State Administrative Employees Association."[13] It would soon become the American Federation of State, County and Municipal Employees, AFSCME, our union.

As expected, the Democrats took control in the 1932 elections.

The *Milwaukee Sentinel* reported on December 23, 1932:

> Repeal of the state civil service law and abolition of the state bureau of personnel will be sought by Democratic leaders as soon as the legislature meets in January. . . . It is necessary to wipe out the entire civil service organization . . . in order to give the state a completely Democratic administration for the next two years.

The *Madison Capital Times* wrote it up in a more colorful way:

HUNGRY DEM HORDES AWAIT SPOILS CHASE:
HAUNT ASSEMBLY GALLERIES FOR
CARROLL BILL PASSAGE[14]

But the existence of the Wisconsin State Employees Association, supported by the American Federation of Labor, changed the nature of the battle from Democrats versus Republicans to Democrats versus Labor, the spoils system versus the civil service. The new union hung on. The civil service program stayed in place.

The president of the new union was Arnold Zander. He was low key, but effective. He began organizing. He out-maneuvered a takeover by the American Federation of Government Employees. He gave the union its national-sounding name, though he ran it with a small budget from Madison, and by the time it was chartered in 1936, as AFSCME, it had 9,737 members.

So AFSCME began in Wisconsin in an effort to stop Democrats from engaging in political cronyism.

It is ironic then that the state in which our union was born has become ground zero in the fight to save workers' rights and the American Dream. In 2010, there was another national electoral sweep that impacted Wisconsin. This time it swept Republicans into office.

They were not Abraham Lincoln's Republicans. You would never hear them say, "Labor is prior to, and independent of, capital. Capital is only the fruit of labor, and could never have existed if labor had not first existed. Labor is the superior of capital, and deserves much the higher consideration." These Republicans routinely refer to people with capital as "job creators," and act as if anyone who gets to work for a "job creator" is being done a favor.

They were not President Theodore Roosevelt's populist Republicans. Can you imagine any of our recent Republican candidates for president declaring, "There is absolutely nothing to be said for government by a plutocracy, for government by men very powerful in certain lines and gifted with 'the money touch,' but with ideals which in their essence are merely those of so many glorified pawnbrokers"?

Or explaining why we need higher income taxes and progressive inheritance taxes, as Theodore Roosevelt did by saying, "The really big fortune, the swollen fortune, by the mere fact of its size acquires qualities which differentiate it in kind as well as in degree from what is possessed by men of relatively small means. Therefore, I believe in a graduated income tax on big fortunes, and in another tax which is far more easily collected and far more effective—a graduated inheritance tax on big fortunes, properly safeguarded against evasion and increasing rapidly in amount with the size of the estate."[15]

These were not even Ronald Reagan Republicans who, despite his actions against air traffic controllers, once famously declared, "Where free unions and collective bargaining are forbidden, freedom is lost."

They were not the progressive or the good government folks of the La Follette tradition. They were a new incarnation of the people that Abe Lincoln, Teddy Roosevelt, and "Fighting Bob" La Follette despised. They were members of a far right, pro-corporate cabal, recipients of lots of corporate funding, some of it openly, some of it in secret. One thing they were sure of: they hated unions.

Their poster boy was the new governor of Wisconsin, Scott Walker.

CHAPTER SEVEN

Meet Scott Walker

HOW'S THIS FOR IRONY? Probably the coldest day I ever went out, actually night I went out, it was twenty-six below, and where do you think there was a water main break? Arctic Avenue."

Brian Stafford has been in the Milwaukee Water Works department for thirty-one years. He's the guy you want fixing a water main break in the cold of winter on Arctic Avenue. Brian was born in Milwaukee. He's got a solid build, with large, thick hands. "What I enjoy about the water department is you're someplace new every day. Just about the time you think you've seen everything, it's 'What the hell?' You learn how to dress. You learn how to tolerate it."

Arctic Avenue is up on the bluff, in a very pleasant residential area, the streets lined with trees, just behind Lake Parkway in Milwaukee. The wind comes in from Lake Michigan, 307 miles long and 30 to 120 miles wide, so it's chilled and damp, and puts an extra edge on the cold night.

"One of the problems in winter is locating the leak. The ground freezes, the water freezes, so where the water surfaces isn't necessarily where the leak is.

"What we do, is we drill small holes and we put a rod down the hole and we listen for the leak. When we get closer to the leak, it gets louder and we keep going until we're sure we're there. We only dig one hole. Nobody wants the streets torn up for blocks, for no good reason. We know what we're doing, one hole.

Courtesy of Joe Lawrence

"An eight-inch water main, that's what most of them are, means about probably three city blocks are out of water because of it. After we locate the leak, we excavate. How we do the repair depends on the break. Ninety percent of the time, we put on a repair clamp, which is exactly what it sounds like: a big patch that goes all the way around. About 10 percent of the time we have to cut the old pipe out and put a new pipe in. That's a much bigger ditch, and a lot more work."

So it's the middle of winter. The wind's coming in off Lake Michigan. Your water's gone out. You can't make coffee, you can't take a hot shower, you only get one flush before the toilet won't operate. You call the city, they send out Brian. It doesn't matter how cold it is. He comes out.

Just as John Kasich blamed it all on BJ, Scott Walker will tell you Brian and some of the other working-class folks you'll meet are the reason the state's in trouble. The only way to save the state is to take the guy who goes out in the middle of the night in Wisconsin in February and bust his union.

Scott Walker was swept into office by the same wave that gave us John Kasich in 2010.

Walker is, in many ways, a Kasich clone. They are both purely political beings.

Walker went to Marquette University. He immediately got involved in politics. Five members of the student council had apparently used student government money for personal expenses. Walker was chairman of the investigating committee. He was playing hardball. The committee recommended impeachment. The accused students resigned. Walker ran for student body president.

The student paper, the *Marquette Tribune*, endorsed his opponent, John Quigley, but noted that both candidates were fit for the office.[1]

But then they retracted that with an editorial entitled "Revision—Walker Unfit." The cause for their reversal was that "a Scott Walker campaign brochure was distributed on campus which amounts to nothing more than a blatant mudslinging spree."[2] The article went on to say that if they had known about it, "We could not have written, in good conscience that Walker would be a good president . . . no one who responds to opposition by distorting (if not assassinating) the character of his opponent and making pouty accusations deserves to be president of the student body."

"Revision—Walker Unfit" was actually published twice.

The first time, "Walker's campaign personnel [were] picking up armfuls of [the] *Tribune* and throwing them away." Walker lost.[3]

He ran again. He lost again.

In 1990, Walker left college. Then he ran for the Wisconsin state assembly. He lost. In 1993 there was a special election coming up in a staunchly Republican district. Walker moved. He ran. He won.

There he stayed for the next nine years. He tried to de-fund public financing for elections while his fellow Republicans were trying to double the tax credit for campaign contributions.

In 2008, the pendulum had swung to the left, in a national effort to get as far from George W. Bush as possible. But by 2010 the pendulum had swung back to the right. Walker saw the opportunity. He ran for governor. He won, swept in with the same wave that brought John Kasich back into politics.

Walker is connected to Kasich at another level as well. They were ALEC fellows.

"Many of us, myself included, were part of ALEC," Walker attested in a Minnesota Public Radio story, called "Corrections, Inc.," about the influence of private prison corporations and ALEC on state legislatures. "Clearly ALEC had proposed model legislation. . . . And probably more important than just the model legislation, [ALEC] had actually put together reports and such that showed the benefits of truth-in-sentencing and showed the successes in other states. And those sorts of statistics were very helpful to us when we pushed it through, when we passed the final legislation."[4]

The Corrections Corporation of America (CCA), the nation's biggest private prison company, and Wackenhut (now

GEO), the second largest, helped write these "model" criminal justice laws to increase the number of people put in prisons and increase their revenue streams.

Wisconsin passed the bill that the private prison industry wrote for ALEC and that ALEC handed off to Scott Walker. From the very start it was costly to the state, but profitable to the people who'd sponsored the legislation.

An "analysis by the state estimated that the 990 inmates imprisoned just in the first 21 months after the law took effect would spend 18,384 additional months in jail, costing taxpayers an extra $41 million.

"That's money in the bank for Corrections Corporation of America, the company that sits on the committee that wrote ALEC's truth-in-sentencing bill. Wisconsin is a CCA customer. Its prisons are overcrowded, so the state houses more than three thousand inmates at CCA facilities in Minnesota, Oklahoma, and Tennessee. The price tag: more than $50 million a year."[5]

In 2011, Scott Walker became governor of Wisconsin. He claimed that the state was in a desperate budget crisis. That crisis made it necessary for him to do desperate things.

Whether that was true or false, at least half a billion dollars of those desperate straits were a direct result of Walker's own policies when he was carrying water for the Corrections Corporation of America.

Scott Walker ran for governor of Wisconsin with a pledge to create two hundred fifty thousand jobs in his first term. He would "implement cuts in manufacturing taxes, estate taxes and retirement taxes. He said those tax reductions could be made with cuts to employee's wages and benefits." That was a reasonable thing to do, because "there's just benefits in particular that are just woefully out of balance with where the private sector is."[6]

Except Walker was wrong. According to a study by Jeffrey Keefe for the Economic Policy Institute in early 2011, "Wisconsin public employees earn 4.8% less in total compensation per hour than comparable full-time employees in Wisconsin's private sector."[7]

Walker was sworn in on January 3, 2011.

In normal times, Wisconsin politics are relatively polite and eminently practical. But there was a new, confrontational atmosphere. Like the incoming governor, the new state senate majority leader, Scott Fitzgerald, was a member of ALEC. So was his brother, the new Speaker of the Assembly. They were excited about the possibilities. At a conference, speaking to the camera, Senator Fitzgerald said:

> I just attended the American Legislative Exchange Council, and I was surprised how much momentum there was . . . nothing like I've ever seen before . . . about some of the major changes that need to happen in and around labor . . . decertifying or Right to Work or other changes . . . both private and public unions.
>
> Listen, we have new majorities, when you talk to the members of the House of the Representatives and the way they view the world right now, the more feathers you ruffle right now the stronger you are going to be politically. And

I don't ever remember an environment where that existed before. You know, it was always get along, nibble on the edges, yeah we would take a few shots here and there at some political enemies, but in the end we all just want to be on the same page. That just doesn't exist right now. I've never seen that before. So I think it gives us a lot of leeway and a lot of chain to make some significant changes.[8]

So the puppet masters from ALEC had taken over Wisconsin. They had an agenda—prepared, prepackaged, and prepaid for thanks to funding from too many major corporations for us to thank right now.

All they needed was a crisis, so they created one with the budget.

Not a big surprise, really. Budget shortfalls had become the crisis du jour.

Here are the numbers. Wisconsin does its budget in two-year June to July cycles. The projection from July 2011 was that there might be a gap of $137 million.

The full 2009–2011 budget, prepared by the previous governor, was $62.7 billion. A shortfall of $137 million is .22 percent. If you think about it, with all the variables in revenues, expenditures, mandates, weather, crime rates, and the thousands of other things that affect the state, being off by just .22 percent is right in the bull's-eye.

As for Walker's own budget—June 2011 through July 2013—he was projecting a $3.6 billion shortfall. That's a big number. All right, .22 percent, even though it's millions of dollars, was not that upsetting. But this, billions of dollars, must be serious, right?

While it's serious enough that it shouldn't be ignored, it was still well within the range of being fixable. In fact, the previous governor had faced a projected deficit of $5.9 billion. He dealt with it.

The crisis was nothing to cry about.

CHAPTER EIGHT

The Real Agenda

Governor Walker and the legislature had a platter of prospective bills written by ALEC in front of them. They were a witches' brew of every pet conservative cause that corporate-backed legislators and lobbyists has been trying to enact in local, state, and federal government for the last two decades.

Here are some of the important ones that passed.

SUPPRESS VOTERS. Under the guise of stopping nearly nonexistent voter fraud, its goal is to make it harder for people to vote if their demographics don't put them in a group inclined to vote the right way.

According to a study by the University of Wisconsin-Milwaukee and highlighted by the Center for Media and Democracy, in Wisconsin, 177,000 people over sixty-five don't have state-issued IDs. "Only 45 percent of African American males and 51 percent of females have a valid drivers license. . . . Student IDs have to be issued from an accredited public or private college, include a student's signature and have a two-year expiration date. The 182,000 . . . students in the University of

Wisconsin system and 300,000 in state technical colleges currently do not meet this requirement."[1]

END PUBLIC FINANCING OF CAMPAIGNS. Wisconsin has had thirty-four years of public financing for elections. That makes it possible for people who want to answer to the public interest instead of to deep-pocket special interests, to run for office. Now that's over with. You have to be a fund-raiser first.

To add insult to injury, that money will be used to help fund the voter ID law intended to keep people from voting.

PRIVATIZE EDUCATION. Several bills targeted public education. The most important was the budget. It cut nearly $1.6 billion over two years from public schools while it opened up funding for charter and private schools.

Milwaukee's voucher program is around twenty years old. That's quite long enough to see if it works. A report by Erin Richards and Amy Hetzner of the *Journal Sentinel* suggested it doesn't: students in Milwaukee's school-choice program performed worse than or about the same as students in Milwaukee's public schools in math and reading, according to statewide tests.[2]

A bill was also introduced to expand virtual schools. These are schools that don't really exist, but get state funds to teach online. They are one of the most lucrative scams to come along since 900 numbers for psychic hotlines. It's called the Charter School Reform Bill.

SLASH TAXES FOR CORPORATIONS WITH OUT-OF-STATE OPERATIONS. This reopens the "Las Vegas loophole" that allows corporations to ship their profits, via accounting tricks, to states with no corporate income tax, such as Nevada. It prohibits the Wisconsin Department of Revenue from challenging certain business tax avoidance strategies. The state will lose over $46 million in the first budget cycle and $40 million per year after that.

BESTOW TAX BREAKS FOR PEOPLE WHO DIDN'T WORK FOR THE MONEY. This eliminates capital gains taxes from investments in Wisconsin. Loss to the state: $79 million once the plan is fully phased in.

BRING BACK PREDATORY LENDING TO THE POOR. Restrictions on payday lenders have been loosened and title loans are back. "Payday and title loans often have annual interest rates that exceed 500%."[3]

HIKE TAXES ON THE POOR. Wisconsin is one of twenty-two states that has an earned-income tax credit that parallels the federal program to help people who work, but don't make much money. While cutting taxes for business, Walker reduced funding for this credit that helps working people.

On August 12, 2011, on MSNBC's *Morning Joe*, Scott Walker said, "I'll be judged on my job creation record."[4]

On December 21, 2011, a Wisconsin Fox station ran with this headline: WISCONSIN LEADS NATION IN JOB LOSSES FOR THE 2ND STRAIGHT MONTH.

The state had lost 14,600 jobs, "the largest over-the-month decrease in employment in the country, followed by Minnesota, which lost 13,700, and Colorado, which lost 4,500."[5]

The *Milwaukee Journal Sentinel* followed up with a story in late January 2012 with an even harsher verdict: "Wisconsin unexpectedly lost private-sector jobs in December for the sixth consecutive month, the same months in which the nation added private sector jobs . . . Losses in the private sector and changes in government staffing left the state with an estimated net loss of 1,700 non-farm jobs for December."[6]

According to an analysis on the job losses by the Center on Wisconsin Strategy, "The second half of 2011 in Wisconsin stands in dramatic and distressing contrast to consistent job growth at the national level. The nation added 853,000 jobs over the last six months of 2011, posting steady growth of 0.7 percent of the job base. Over those same six months Wisconsin lost 35,600 jobs, bringing the job base down by just over 1 percent. *No other state lost that many jobs*."[7]

Here's another comparison of Walker's Wisconsin with the rest of the United States.

The Federal Reserve Bank of Philadelphia produces something called a coincident index. It rolls non-farm payroll employment, average hours worked in manufacturing, the unemployment rate, and wage and salary disbursements deflated by the consumer price index into a single statistic.[8]

The index shows that since Walker's budget went into effect in July 2011, Wisconsin has delivered the worst performance in the nation. (See map on page 80.)

And here is the kicker about Walker's claims that he needed to do away with collective bargaining rights to fix budget

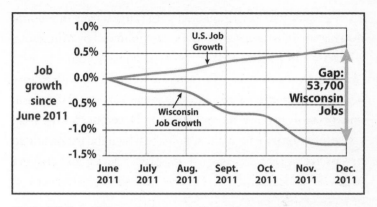

Under Walker, Wisconsin Is 53,700 Jobs Short of Matching the National Pace of Job Creation

Source: Graph courtesy of Institute for Wisconsin's Future. http://www.wisconsinsfuture.org.

shortfalls. Scott Walker included the anti-union language in a "budget repair" bill when he discovered that the state faced a $137 million budget shortfall. In February 2012, Wisconsin's nonpartisan Legislative Fiscal Bureau announced that Walker's own budget contained a $143 million shortfall. This time though, Walker said no budget repair bill was necessary. Governor Walker said that stealing union rights would fix a budget shortfall. It didn't. Now Walker has a shortfall even larger than the one he used as a ruse to steal workers' rights, and he says no legislative action is needed.

Scott Walker is a charlatan selling a bill of free market goods. We know his job creation plans were phony. We know his concerns about deficit reduction were unfounded because he gave tax breaks to corporations, which meant less revenue. But if you don't believe us, take it from Walker himself.

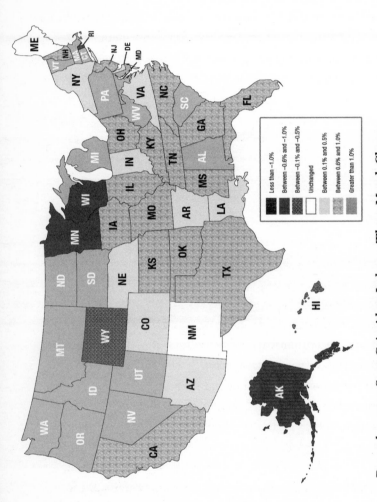

December 2011 State Coincident Indexes: Three-Month Change

Source: Federal Reserve Bank of Philadephia.

Ian Murphy is a citizen journalist who writes for The Beast website (buffalobeast.com). During the protests in Madison, state Senator Tim Carpenter gave an interview to the *Huffington Post* expressing frustration that Scott Walker wouldn't meet with or return phone calls from any of the members of the Democratic senate caucus, including Carpenter, who had left Wisconsin in protest of Walker's scheme to ram his anti-union bill through the legislature.

If Walker wouldn't take calls from elected senators, who would he take a call from? Murphy wondered. That's when Murphy called Walker's office under the persona of billionaire David Koch—the same David Koch of class warfare fame. Walker took the call.

For twenty minutes, Scott Walker laid forth in astonishing detail to "David Koch" his plan to break public service unions. Walker said he had "layoff notices ready" for five thousand to six thousand state workers that he was prepared to send out to "ratchet up" the political pressure to bust public service unions. He told "Koch" of his plan to trick senate Democrats into returning with a promise to talk, only to ram the bill through once they returned since he had no plan to compromise. He admitted to considering a Nixonian plan to plant troublemakers in the crowds. And he reminisced over a meeting he had with his cabinet members on the eve of his union-busting scheme:

> I stood up and I pulled out a picture of Ronald Reagan, and I said, you know, this may seem a little melodramatic, but 30 years ago, Ronald Reagan, whose 100th birthday we just celebrated the day before, had one of the most defining moments of his political career, not just his pres-

idency, when he fired the air-traffic controllers. And, uh, I said, to me that moment was more important than just for labor relations or even the federal budget, that was the first crack in the Berlin Wall and the fall of Communism because from that point forward, the Soviets and the Communists knew that Ronald Reagan wasn't a push-over. And, uh, I said this may not have as broad of world implications, but in Wisconsin's history—little did I know how big it would be nationally—in Wisconsin's history, I said this is our moment, this is our time to change the course of history.[9]

Scott Walker's real agenda had nothing to do with Wisconsin's budget. It had everything to do with petty politics, just as it did when he was at Marquette University. Scott Walker was a man on a political mission to "change the course of history," and he would take out Brian Stafford, the guy out at 2:00 a.m. fixing broken water pipes in the dead of winter, and anyone else who stood in his way.

CHAPTER NINE

On, Wisconsin!

LATONYA JOHNSON is a licensed home child-care provider in Milwaukee.

She was born in Le Grange, Tennessee, in 1979. She grew up in a shack without running water and moved to Milwaukee to live with her grandfather when she was twelve years old. Her family thought there would be more opportunity up in Wisconsin. Her two aunts and her two cousins all lived with him, too. "He took care of all of us. We thought he was rich. Now I understand, all he had was a good union job."

LaTonya earned a degree in criminal justice from Tennessee State University. Two weeks after graduation, her daughter was born prematurely. She moved back to Wisconsin two months later, once her daughter was able to travel. LaTonya tried being a telemarketer, a caseworker for Wisconsin Works, the state's program to move people from welfare to employment, and she had her own insurance agency. Eventually she realized that she wanted to help kids. She was faced with the problem that all working parents face: how to find enough time for both a job and children.

She opened a home day-care center, which meant that she could be with her daughter while she earned a living. LaTonya takes care of the children and she does it around the clock. Two of the children in her care have a mother who works the third shift, midnight to eight in the morning, full time, and part time on the first shift, starting at eight in the morning. The children get dropped off a little before midnight, put back to bed, then LaTonya gets them up in the morning and gets them ready for school.

Courtesy of Joe Lawrence

As an employer, government can be as tough and mean and cheap as any private corporation. The child-care subsidy was originally set at 75 percent of the market rate in the immediate community. In theory, the parents were supposed to contribute a co-pay to make up the difference. In reality it proved impossible for child-care providers to collect extra money from people with jobs that paid minimum wage, or very close to it, and needed food stamps just to get by. The rate the state pays has not been revised in years. Now it's closer to 63 percent of the market rate.

Schools, both private and public, are reimbursed on the basis of enrollment, but home child-care providers only get paid for the days when children show up. If children get sick or go to visit their grandparents, or their own parents are sick and can't get them to child care, then certified and licensed family providers don't get paid.

The rules that the state set for this kind of day care filled a two-and-a-half-inch binder. They'd been written with no input from providers, the people who would have to apply them and live with them. Rules and rates could be changed at the whim of the state. Participating providers could be eliminated from the program without due cause and without the means to appeal, short of hiring a lawyer and going to court, by which time they'd be out of business.

At last, in 2006, Governor Jim Doyle, a Democrat, signed an executive order that allowed home child-care providers to form a union. AFSCME organizers and local child-care providers went out, door-to-door, and signed people up. The 2009–2010 state budget formalized recognition of the union.

For LaTonya, having a union wasn't about money or benefits. It was about dignity and respect. With a union she had a way to speak to power, so that someone would actually have to listen.

In 2011, Scott Walker took all that away from LaTonya. He took away her right to have a union. It's impossible to argue that it was about the state's solvency when people weren't even being paid market rate. It was to make sure that she had no way to talk back to power. It was a way to silence her ten-dollar influence on politics while the Koch brothers got the right to spend without limit.

Wisconsin's child-care providers, nurses, EMTs, correctional officers, and other public service workers knew that Scott Walker was no friend. But few thought he would actually seek to demolish union freedom. On February 9, 2011, the Isthmus's *Daily Page* blogger David Blaska, in a post titled "R.I.P. Wisconsin Government Employee Unions," broke the news that a bill doing just that would be introduced that Friday. Blaska gleefully advised public employee union leaders to update their resumes, and argued that "public employee unions have used up their good will among the public."

Scott Walker formally introduced Senate Bill 11 on Monday, February 14. Walker folded the language eliminating collective bargaining rights into a so-called "budget repair" bill—legislation that he said was needed to close Wisconsin's budget shortfall. Walker said he considered SB11 an emergency bill and recommended that it be passed before the budget bill.

Judging from many of the headlines in early February, one might be convinced that Governor Walker's approach was rather benign; common sense belt-tightening reforms. A typical example is this February 4 headline in the *Appleton Post-Crescent*: GOVERNOR WALKER PUSHES FOR REFORMS THAT GIVE MUNICIPALITIES MORE CONTROL. Who could argue with that?

But when people saw that the bill actually denied union rights, things changed. As president and secretary-treasurer of the national union, we began talking to our local leaders and offering support. We knew what this meant for public service workers in Wisconsin. Marty Beil, Rick Badger, and Rich Abelson, who together represented more than sixty thousand public service workers, were united and ready for the fight, despite Scott Walker's promises to "David Koch" that he wouldn't compromise.

On Friday afternoon, we received an email titled "What this means," written by a member in Wisconsin, which in gut-wrenching detail described the mood among workers in a local public office: "It is really bad. The worst I've ever seen. We have a secretary who will not be able to make it on these cuts. She has one teenage daughter and is a single mom. It's heartbreaking watching staff today." Struggling secretaries like this single mother are who Indiana Governor Mitch Daniels, who made millions in the pharmaceutical industry, referred to in 2010 as part of a "privileged class" of public service workers in America.

We knew we had to stand up and fight back.

The weekend of February 11, community leaders throughout the state held numerous press events to educate reporters and the public about what was really at stake. Wisconsinites published op-eds and letters to the editor. They launched television and radio ads. Mary Bell, a Madison librarian and president of the Wisconsin Education Association Council, and Phil Neuenfeldt, president of the Wisconsin AFL-CIO, put compelling faces and voices to the issue in press conferences. All with one simple message: Public employees were willing to make concessions, but they'd be damned if they were going to give up their union rights.

One press conference even featured conservative and Republican workers arguing that Walker's bill was anathema to conservative thinking. Bob Jahn, a highway worker from Green Lake, said, "I'm a proud conservative because I believe in limited government, especially when it comes to the government's intrusion on individual rights. This anti-freedom scheme being rammed through the legislature goes against every core conservative principle there is." DON'T TREAD ON ME and IT'S ABOUT FREEDOM! signs populated the rallies.[1]

It has been suggested that this was a prime reason why attempted counter-protests organized by Tea Party leaders supporting Walker flopped. Tea Partiers apparently didn't believe that the government should take away an individual's freedom any more than we did.

Though tactical plans were hastily drawn in frantic meetings throughout the weekend, the intensity of the outcry was spontaneous. Madison is the state capital and the location of the main campus of the University of Wisconsin. It's a city with a population of nearly 235,000 and more than fifty thousand college students. Peter Rickman, a student at the University of Wisconsin and a rank-and-file leader of the Teaching Assistants' Association, was at the center of it. "What happened in Madison was not an accident," he said. "The real story is about months of building a student-worker alliance. Of organizing to be ready for flash-points."[2]

Following the ALEC blueprint, Walker took away collective bargaining rights of University of Wisconsin employees, including professors and teaching assistants. But they brought something special to the fight. As academics and university employees they saw it in broader terms. The assault on public education, the assault on the university, and the assault on unions were all connected, part of the class war being waged by the wealthy against the American Dream.

Students started mobilizing as soon as rumors of the bill started floating around campus. By the time the governor handed the bill to the legislators, the students were quickly working through their networks. They phoned, texted, emailed, tweeted, and posted messages on Facebook. There was a rally at the student union on Saturday. It was just fifty to seventy-five people, hardly heralding what was to come. But they met, and they planned along with hundreds of others around the state. Here are excerpts from one action alert that was circulated that weekend:

Four Things We Need to Do to Win

1. DAYS OF ACTION We need you at all of these actions this week. If you can only make one or two, we understand—but we really need as many people as possible at all of them, because this fight is so critical.

2. CALL YOUR LEGISLATORS We need to generate thousands of calls to state legislators asking them to oppose Walker's bill. Elected representatives must hear from people to know that this bill simply is the wrong thing to do to public service workers and the people they serve. It is crucial that you contact the legislators both from your hometown in Wisconsin and from your current address.

3. MOBILIZE OTHERS TO CONTACT LEGISLATORS One of the keys to winning this fight is to spread out far and wide the recruitment of people to contact legislators. We need you to get into contact with everyone you know in Wisconsin to make the phone call of our lives.

(a) Forward the Email Forward this email and set of instructions to everyone in your email contact list that lives in or comes from Wisconsin. If you are on listserves, send it along too. And ask everyone in your email to send along to other individuals and listserves.

(b) Call Through Your Contact List Emails can help reach people, but a live, active contact makes all the difference.

(c) Talk to Friends, Family, Co-Workers Those closest to you or who most similarly share your situation are most likely to take immediate, concrete action. Make a special, concerted, personally ask of these people to make the calls and recruit others to do so as well.

4. WRITE A LETTER TO THE EDITOR These legislators need to hear in public forums like newspaper editorial boards that people oppose this extreme bill. We need to generate letters to the editor of local newspapers in targeted State Senate districts.[3]

That was exactly what they did.

On Monday, over one thousand students packed the statehouse. Even doing something as "loving" as delivering valentines led to the capitol floors shaking.

They came back on Tuesday. But now it was more than just students. Workers, too, both in the public sector and the private sector, joined them. Twenty thousand in all. They made their way into the hearing room, and they demanded to be heard. They packed the statehouse, and when the building was full, they gathered outside on the lawns.

The Republicans tried to shut the hearings down. There was a people's revolt. They insisted on the right to speak. They refused to leave.

Both of us were in Madison that day. And what we witnessed was one of the most inspiring events of our lives. Capitol rallies tend to run the gamut from stunning success if there are five thousand people and three TV cameras to total flops. That's thirty people and a reporter who showed up by accident. This was unlike anything we had ever seen. As we approached the podium for an afternoon press conference, we noticed that the attendance was so overwhelming that there literally was no space to set up cameras, and reporters had to wedge themselves into the crowd wherever they found a spot.

Though a few professionally made signs dotted the landscape, the vast majority were homemade: hand-scribbled slogans on poster board urging lawmakers inside to KILL THE BILL and urging folks to PROTEST LIKE AN EGYPTIAN. And students made sure their unique imprimatur was noticed through some pretty creative signage. One sign some fifty yards away read JUSTIN BIEBER SAYS HELL NO! with a huge cutout of the teen pop icon's smiling face.

And though Madison was the epicenter of the action, the protests were statewide and local, from Green Bay to Milwaukee to La Crosse to Eau Claire to Wausau. Janice Bobholz, an information specialist with the Dodge County sheriff's department, attended a protest in her town the night that Walker introduced his bill.

Forty-five miles from Madison, in Horicon, Wisconsin, Bobholz told the two hundred protesters, "Walker underestimates the fact that belonging to a union is what makes us strong." Throughout the next several weeks, Bobholz spoke at rallies, testified to lawmakers, and appeared on television. She also talked to rural folks in Dodge County, educating them about how Walker's bill "cut services to farmers, the elderly and the less fortunate."

Tuesday, February 15, was also the day that Wisconsin media started to tell the real story behind Walker's scheme, a result of all the work that community leaders had done the weekend before. That morning, as those twenty thousand Wisconsinites crowded the capitol, the *Milwaukee Journal Sentinel*'s front-page headline blared: RIGHTS, NOT BENEFITS, AT ISSUE. Contrary to Blaska's assertion, the public quickly came to understand what this fight was about—and they were with public service workers. It was the turning point.

Something was happening in Wisconsin, something led by working and middle-class Wisconsinites who had had enough. And it felt good. Adam Sutter, a corrections officer from Prairie du Chien, came to Madison for the protests "to protect my rights as a worker, to have a seat at the bargaining table, and for my kids and their kids." He needed his children to see what was happening in response to Walker's attacks. "I told my children we are a movement, we are making history."

At first, the national media paid very little attention. One exception was Bill O'Reilly, who took it very seriously indeed and ran a clip of protesters rudely shoving someone, with what looked like rioting, behind him. There were also palm trees in the footage. For those who might not know Wisconsin's climate well, palm trees don't grow there. O'Reilly's weak attempt to portray the peaceful protesters as violent rioters became a laughingstock. Protesters in Wisconsin even started bringing inflatable palm trees and beach gear to the February rallies.

Thankfully, social media filled the initial void. Facebook and Twitter were alive with news from Wisconsin. Ian's Pizza, a local pizza joint just off the capitol square, began getting donations from around the world to feed the protesters. For weeks, Ian's provided the fuel—including an "only in Wisconsin" macaroni-and-cheese-covered pizza—for a budding movement. Ian's even received donations from Egypt, where thousands of protesters had taken to the streets to demand democracy. Despite the life-or-death risk of protesting in Egypt, people there found the time to stand in solidarity with their sisters and brothers in Madison.

As a side note, while one is hard-pressed to make a direct comparison between Scott Walker and former Egyptian dictator Hosni Mubarak, it did not go unnoticed that as thousands marched for freedom in Egypt, their American brothers and sisters marched to stop Governor Walker's anti-freedom power grab.

In July, Egyptian youth activist Sarah Kamal of the April 6 Youth Movement spoke at our Next Wave conference, an AFSCME initiative to equip the next generation of union leaders. During an interview with Tim Birkley, one of the young AFSCME leaders who organized overnight protests in the state capitol, Kamal said, "Egypt sent a message to all the world that everything is possible to do, if we dream and we work together in a systematic way, we can do anything we hope for."

MSNBC's Ed Schultz helped spread the story nationally, declaring, "There is no bigger story than what is unfolding in Wisconsin." He broadcast live from the protest site, and often hosted respected author and progressive political pundit John Nichols, who, as a Madison resident, told the story from the ground as few could.

Thanks to social media and the new national exposure, the Wisconsin protests spread nationwide, a warning shot to other governors and legislatures not to follow Scott Walker's lead. On the other side of the country, health-care providers held a candlelight vigil to protest Walker's anti-worker power grab. "This is about protecting our rights," said Laura Reyes, president of the United Domestic Workers of America, at the vigil in Orange County. "The workers in Wisconsin fought long and hard for bargaining rights and I'll be damned if they are going to take them from me."

Huge crowds gathered in Ohio where John Kasich had indeed chosen to follow Walker and was trying to break the public service unions. Scott Walker gave a telephone interview to Bloomberg News in which he said Kasich had called him for advice. According to Walker, he told Kasich, "Don't blink." Walker also told "David Koch" that he was in touch with Kasich daily.

The creative community was watching, too. Actress and activist Susan Sarandon said Wisconsin was "a wakeup call for all of America in the 21st century that builds upon the legacy of unions." Actor Tony Shalhoub called Wisconsin the birth of "a nationwide movement destined to restore the rights of workers, to safeguard quality education for our children and to re-assemble and reconstitute the fragmented and wounded middle class."[4]

Taking to Twitter, as several musicians and actors did to express their outrage, actor Mark Ruffalo wrote: "Conservative Gov. scapegoats the workers for his corporate tax breaks then uses deficit to break the back of the unions. It's BS."[5]

Former Rage Against the Machine guitarist and current Nightwatchman Tom Morello and Dropkick Murphys lent their voices and talents to the struggle. Supporting workers' rights, which the corporate-backed right had told America was a thing of the past, was cool again.

But even with tens of thousands of his constituents occupying the statehouse, Walker refused to compromise. He wasn't even going to talk. The Republicans had a clear majority in the Senate: 19–14. They voted in lockstep. They insisted the bill would pass by the weekend. Despite the growing protests and evidence to the contrary, Governor Walker stuck to his talking point that this was primarily a battle over money, an attempt to rein in out-of-control, and unfair, health and welfare costs. It wasn't.

AFSCME leaders in Wisconsin made the decision with other public service union leaders to accept increased pension and health-care contributions, exactly what Scott Walker said needed to be done to balance the budget. Walker said no dice. He refused to sit down at the table to find a solution. As he told "David Koch" during that infamous prank phone call, he had no interest in doing so. He wanted to bust the unions.

Walker's decision to include the union-busting legislation in a so-called budget repair bill would come back to haunt him.

Matters of money required a quorum of at least twenty senators to vote. At that time, the chamber was made up of nineteen Republicans and fourteen Democrats. On Thursday morning, February 17, all fourteen of the Democratic state senators disappeared, denying Walker the chance to ram through the budget bill.

The Senate majority leader, Scott Fitzgerald, called his father to go and get the missing senators back. Just a few days before the union-busting bill was introduced, Walker appointed Stephen Fitzgerald, the father of Scott and Jeff, the Speaker of the Assembly, as head of the Wisconsin State Patrol.

State troopers were dispatched in the hope that some of the Democrats were still in the state and could be hauled back to the state capitol building. They only needed one.

The protesters were jubilant when they learned that all fourteen of the senators made it across the state line to Illinois.

By Saturday, February 19, seventy thousand people crowded the capitol. Something had gone very, very wrong with Scott Walker's attempts to divide and conquer. If anything, he had succeeded in uniting people against a bill that everyone now knew had nothing to do with the budget and everything to do with attacking the working middle class. People came from the steel mills and the paper mills. There were autoworkers, machinists, students, retirees, LGBT (lesbian, gay, bisexual, and transgender) advocates, clergy, and farmers. The air was filled with the sound of taxi drivers honking their horns in support.

Though police officers and firefighters were exempt from the bill, they came in a show of solidarity. Throughout the week, firefighters, bagpipes and drums in tow, marched around the capitol in their uniforms. "We could have stood idly by," said

Mahlon Mitchell, the president of the Professional Fire Fighters of Wisconsin. "After talking with my membership, we decided that we had to act. An assault on one is really an assault on all. . . . Now we have a fire in the house of labor, there's a fire in our house, and we're going to put the fire out! . . . We have to be clear, this is not just an attack on unions, this is an attack on the middle class."[6]

The firefighters and the police even offered to make the same adjustments to their pensions and health care as the other public service employees, even though they didn't have to, if it meant everyone kept their collective-bargaining rights.

On February 26, MoveOn.org and other progressive allies organized solidarity protests across the country. Tens of thousands from New York to California rallied in opposition to attacks against collective-bargaining rights, and in general the continuing assault on the nation's working middle class.

Increasingly unnerved that their plans for quick passage had gone awry, and taking a daily beating in the media both within and outside Wisconsin, Walker and Republican legislative leaders decided they had had enough. On March 9, state senate leaders took that so-called budget repair bill and stripped it of anything having to do with the budget. All that remained was the language outlawing the freedom to collectively bargain.

In effect, Walker was admitting that the anti-union provisions had nothing to do with money or the budget, which meant that no quorum was necessary to pass it.

The anti-union bill passed the senate floor 18–1. (Republican state Senator Dale Schultz refused to support the bill.) No Democratic senators were present. The state assembly passed it the next day as chants of "Shame! Shame! Shame!" thundered throughout the occupied capitol. With Walker's signature, it became law.

The hundreds of thousands of Wisconsinites who opposed Governor Walker's anti-freedom bill could be forgiven if at this point they had thrown up their hands and accepted defeat. But the Madison protests had become much more than a legislative fight between pro-union and anti-union legislators. It became a rallying cry for the American Dream—the moment when working people said "Enough!" to corporate-backed politicians, to David and Charles Koch, to ALEC, and everyone else who for decades has waged a class war against them.

Despite the bill's passage, March 12 saw the largest rally to date, with over a hundred thousand Wisconsinites welcoming home the "Wisconsin 14," the name given to the fourteen brave state senators who decided their job was to protect freedom, not take it away. The feeling in the crowd was electric, the applause deafening. The sight of farmers driving their tractors to the capitol mall was unforgettable.

Yes, Scott Walker and his allies had won the legislative battle. Yes, Brian Stafford and LaTonya Johnson had been disenfranchised. And yes, difficult fights, including recalls of state senators on both sides of the aisle, lay ahead. But on that cold, sunny Saturday, Wisconsinites from all walks of life—urban and rural, union and nonunion, black, white, Hispanic, gay, straight, rich and poor—stood in solidarity unbroken and unbowed. Main Street had its voice back.

CHAPTER TEN

The Buckeye Barrage

LEE EICHER is a meat inspector. Her job as a compliance officer is to go into local stockyards and meat processing plants to make sure the animals are healthy, that they are handled and slaughtered humanely, that the facilities are sanitary, and that regulations are being followed. She inspects everything from beef and chicken to venison and buffalo. She is methodical and thorough and she keeps us safe. That's an important responsibility.

But Ohio's Governor Kasich says he wants to run government, including Eicher's job, like a business.

"How can you run meat inspection like a business?" she wonders. "What revenue is there? It's like being a sheriff's deputy, or the state patrol."

Eicher is a member of the Ohio Civil Service Employees Association. She remembers when she and her colleagues often had to pay for the equipment and tools they needed to do their jobs safely and effectively, because the government wouldn't provide it. That's before they had a union.

"The union got us hard hats and steel-toed shoes. We fought for hazardous duty pay for the slaughter-house that's in a prison. I mean you're in a plant with prisoners carrying knives, large, sharp knives, and there's a safe cage for in-spectors to jump in and lock themselves in for protection if things get out of hand. Isn't that worth a few extra dollars, just for the stress?"

Courtesy of Lee Eicher

With her years of experience and education, Eicher could leave for a higher-paying job in the private sector. But she prefers where she is now. "I make sure the people I love, the people I grew up with, and the people of Ohio are protected."

Others were worried less about the people of Ohio eating untainted meat and more about busting Lee's union. It seemed the stars were aligned to let them. Newly elected Governor Ka-sich had solid majorities in the house and senate. Like Scott Walker, John Kasich believed the opportunity was ripe to pit "taxpayers" against "public service workers."

Yet Kasich's Senate Bill 5, which basically took away col-lective bargaining rights of public workers, was not an easy bill to pass. Not a single Democrat supported it. Sure, that was ex-pected. But what wasn't expected was that not even all Repub-licans, known for message discipline and voting in lockstep, could stomach the bill. "Senate President Tom Niehaus was

forced to yank two GOP dissenters from Senate committees . . .
so the bill could move to the floor for a full vote."[1]

One of those dissenters, state Senator Bill Seitz, was
stripped of his chairmanship of the Senate Government Over-
sight Committee and thrown off a second committee. "They
had to take me off the committee because the committee was
deadlocked six-to-six, and six-to-six doesn't pass legislation,"
Seitz said.[2]

As they had in Wisconsin, thousands of men, women, and
children flooded Ohio's statehouse grounds, protesting Senate
Bill 5. The leaders of our AFSCME affiliates in Ohio, Joe Ru-
gola, JoAnn Johntony, John Lyall, Chris Mabe, and International Vice President Eddie Parks, were working the phones
and mobilizing thousands of members. Tens of thousands of e-
mails and postcards arrived in senate offices, imploring lawmakers to oppose the bill. Switchboards jammed with calls. As
the weeks went on, the numbers grew outside the capitol, as
did the tension inside.

The Republican majority in the Senate was 23–10. Getting
this thing passed on the floor should have been a Sunday stroll.
But six Republicans deserted. There was a lot of arm-twisting,
and Kasich finally shoved the bill through, 17–16. The minute
it passed the senate, it was rushed over to the house, where it
passed immediately. It all happened so quickly, the legal staff at
AFSCME Ohio Council 8 actually had to explain the bill's con-
tents to legislators because very few even knew what was in it.

Watching it get rammed through in the senate, protesters
began chanting "Shame on you!" in the house chamber; the citizens who had made it inside chanted and booed, disgusted by
what they were watching unfold. As a parting shot, they were

ordered out of the chamber as House Speaker William Batchelder mocked them, remarking derisively into a microphone, "Now that the intellectuals have left the chamber . . ."[3]

Representative Dan Ramos, in his first year as a state legislator, was in disbelief as the law passed. "There are no redeeming or thoughtful qualities to the legislation they are putting forward. If this majority had its way, this state would have two classes of people: their billion-dollar buddies and the working poor."[4]

On March 31, Kasich signed his pet bill into law.

BJ Simmons-Talley had been disenfranchised. Lee Eicher had been disenfranchised. The men and women of Ohio had been silenced.

With passage of Senate Bill 5, workers were stripped of their rights. They couldn't discuss staffing levels or safety measures at all. BJ suddenly found herself back in the 1970s, when she'd started driving a school bus with no collective bargaining; the days when women went back to driving school buses two days after they had a baby because they were scared to lose their jobs.

Under Kasich's new law, unions could "discuss" employment terms, working conditions, and wages. But if they didn't reach an agreement, they couldn't go to arbitration; all they could do was accept management's offer.

More high-profile conservatives started coming out against the anti-union scheme. Conservative radio and television host Bill Cunningham, a Kasich supporter, appeared on *The Ed Show* and said the result of SB5 would be "collective begging" instead of collective bargaining. "Let's say that you and your lovely wife . . . are in divorce court and you don't agree on the custody of the kids. How would you feel if your wife put on the robe, went up to the bench, and ruled on your case. . . . At the end of the day, if there's not an agreement, the position of the management is imposed on the workers."[5]

But Kasich forgot about one thing: his own state's constitution.

The Constitution of the State of Ohio gives power to the people; it allows for initiatives to enact laws and for citizens to veto them at the ballot box.

If the governor signs a law that the citizens don't like, Ohioans have ninety days to go out and get signatures on a petition to put the law on the ballot. They need a number equivalent to 6 percent of the number of voters who voted in the last election for governor. Based on the 2010 gubernatorial election, BJ needed two hundred thirty thousand signatures, plus a few more in case any were ruled invalid. If she and her friends could get enough signatures, the law would be suspended until the next election. Then the voters could approve it or veto it.

And believe us, BJ planned to give Ohio voters that chance. She and her union and nonunion sisters and brothers in the Buckeye State started knocking on doors and getting people to sign petitions. During the next three months, more than ten thousand citizens joined her, fanning out across the Buckeye State with clipboards. They went to farmers markets and churches. They set up drive-through signature stations, where folks didn't even have to leave their cars to take a stand. They could just drive up to a parking lot where a volunteer was waiting with a petition and pen. A Cleveland hot dog vender kept a petition booklet on his cart and collected from lunchtime customers. A retired teacher living in a nursing home sent out invitations asking friends and family to come celebrate her ninetieth birthday by stopping by and signing her petition booklet.

James Adkins, a corrections officer and union member in Richwood, Ohio, drove more than three thousand miles that spring and summer, collecting nearly two thousand signatures. He gave up turkey hunting. There was a bigger quarry that season. Adkins only set out to get a thousand petition signatures but kept on driving, racking up twice as many, "When just as many Republicans as Democrats were telling me that SB 5 went too far."

While James was out getting signatures, we were marshaling the strength and resources of AFSCME, combining them with those of like-minded organizations and community leaders. Local leaders and citizens formed a coalition called We Are Ohio, modeled after the successful local We Are Wisconsin effort in that state, dedicated to protecting workers' rights and the American Dream. Dedicated to getting those petition signatures.

On June 29, under a brilliant blue sky, more than six thousand We Are Ohio volunteers marched alongside a forty-eight-foot-long semi-truck in what was called "The People's Parade" through downtown Columbus to deliver their signatures to the secretary of state. They needed 230,000. Being hauled inside that semi were 1,298,301.

There were 1,502 boxes of petitions in all, all processed and kept safe under the watchful eye of guards in the days leading up to the delivery. Engineers had to check the structural integrity of the secretary of state's office floor, to ensure it would hold all of them.

It would. And we stacked up every last box. The right of public service workers to have a union would go on the ballot for a vote on November 8.

Lee Eicher would have her vote to repeal SB5, now called Issue 2 after it was placed on the ballot. "If you think you can walk on us, think again."

BJ Simmons-Talley would have her vote. "Main Street is taking this country back."[6]

But we had even more work to do to defeat Issue 2. We had doors to knock on. We had phone calls to make. We had leaflets to deliver. Morning. Noon. Night.

We knew the opponents of workers and the middle class weren't going to just roll over. Kasich would fight back. And almost immediately, out-of-state money was pouring in from Citizens United, the Alliance for American Future, the Republican Governors Association, Dick Cheney's daughter, and Karl Rove. It was a reunion only ALEC could love, and they'd brought their checkbooks.

David Bossie, president of Citizens United, the far right organization whose landmark Supreme Court case in 2010 opened the floodgates to corporate money in politics, chipped in $2.5 million on an ad buy toward the end of the campaign. Bossie probably knew at that point it was a lost cause but, as he told the *Columbus Dispatch*, defeating union rights wasn't his real goal: "We believe, from a 30,000-feet view, that every single one of these races is connected to defeating Barack Obama next November."[7]

While we felt confident that Governor Kasich had gone way too far, victory on Issue 2 was far from certain. Collective bargaining as a stand-alone issue had never been on a statewide ballot before. Kasich was betting, as Scott Walker did, that public service workers had, as David Blaska put it in his post, "used up their good will among the public."[8] Polling throughout the campaign showed that we had reason for optimism, but it was by no means a slam dunk. In fact, a September Quinnipiac poll that showed our support slipping to a bare majority of 51 percent caused some concern.

But then Kasich's team made a major blunder. It became known as "Grannygate." And if there's one group of people you can be sure will never use up their good will among the public, it's grandmas.

CHAPTER ELEVEN

Victory in Ohio

WE ARE OHIO, the pro-workers' rights coalition, ran a television ad in the closing weeks of the campaign featuring Marlene Quinn, a woman from Cincinnati whose great-granddaughter Zoey was rescued by Ohio firefighters during a 2010 house fire. Quinn argued that without collective bargaining, firefighters would not have the ability to negotiate for proper staffing levels. Behind a photo of a firefighter carrying her great-granddaughter's limp body down a ladder from the burning house, Quinn explained, "If it weren't for the firefighters, Zoey wouldn't be with us today." Then, underneath footage of Quinn playing on the swings with her vibrant great-granddaughter, she said, "That's why it's so important to vote no on Issue 2 . . . Fewer firefighters can mean the difference between life and death."[1]

That powerful ad pretty much summed up what Issue 2 meant for Ohioans. Public service workers, including firefighters, know better than politicians how to keep our communities safe, healthy, and strong. Denying them the freedom to collectively bargain would hurt their ability to do so.

Lacking effective messengers for their arguments, Building a Better Ohio, the anti-worker coalition supporting Kasich's law, decided to steal Quinn's voice for their own. In their version of the ad, they used Quinn's anguish about Zoey, but then deceptively replaced her call to vote no with a voiceover saying, "Vote yes on Issue 2." The lawyer for Building a Better Ohio defended the move, saying that seventy-eight-year-old great-grandma Marlene was fair game because, "The woman featured in the ad chose to make herself a public figure by participating in a paid advertisement."[2] Kasich agreed, saying of Building a Better Ohio's ad, "What they're doing is fine."[3]

TV stations statewide saw it differently. Alerted to the dishonesty of the ad and bombarded with calls and e-mails from angry viewers, all thirty-four stations pulled it within two days.

Marlene Quinn saw it differently, too. She was attending church camp when the controversy erupted. But when she returned, she made her displeasure known. She called the ad "dishonest and downright deceitful" and told the media she felt "violated." She also appeared in a second ad for We Are Ohio, this time saying, "The organization behind Issue 2 stole my words to make it seem like I support Issue 2. I don't. They must be desperate to twist the words of a grandma just to get their way. Don't let the politicians put our communities at risk. Vote no on Issue 2."[4]

But it wasn't just television ads that helped Ohioans to see Issue 2 for what it was. It was also about shoe leather and phone calls. Church meetings and knocking on doors.

Lee Saunders was born and raised in Cleveland, Ohio, so this fight was personal for him. He spent weeks, including the final days of the campaign, traveling around the state meeting with volunteers, phone banking, and knocking on doors.

Hearing the reactions from people door-to-door, an increasing sense of optimism that voters would overturn the anti-worker law set in. House to house, neighbor to neighbor, leaves crunching beneath volunteers' feet between each visit, the story was the same: "I'm voting no on Issue 2 because I'm tired of the attacks on the working middle class!" "I'm voting no on Issue 2 because my cousin is a teacher and she deserves the same rights as anyone else!" "I'm voting no on Issue 2 because if we let them take out the middle class, we won't recognize Ohio in another couple years!"

By Election Day, the question wasn't so much whether the citizens of Ohio would overturn Issue 2, but by how much. Unlike some recent election nights, it didn't take long to find out. When all was said and done, Issue 2 was defeated 61–39 percent, a landslide. It was declared "a tremendous victory for the middle class and working families" in the media. It certainly was.[5]

And not just in Ohio.

David Levine is twenty-seven, supporting his wife and their two-year-old son in Pittsburgh on the salary he makes working for the state of Pennsylvania. His job is helping folks navigate the application system for food stamps and other public assistance programs. That salary is $29,000—about $558 a week, before taxes.

"It's funny," says Levine. "We're actually eligible for public assistance."

Every month brings more demands on that $558. There's the $610 for the rent he pays for his family's small apartment and an electric bill that always seems to top $150. There are groceries to buy and diapers, too. Lots of them.

Courtesy of Luis Gomez

Levine is an affable guy who roots for the Steelers in the fall and the Pirates in the summer. He's got the right personality for dealing with ever-swelling caseloads and the increasingly anxious men and women coming now to the state for help, some for the first time ever because of the recession. People who have held the same job for twenty years who suddenly find themselves out of work, needing food stamps and money for medical expenses and utility bills. At least two hundred of them come through the door each day.

"People who have never asked for a dime are now in a mess, wondering how they're going to put clothes on their backs and feed their families," says Levine.

So Levine works the phones at his office downtown all day, fielding calls and working appeals through the system, ensuring they get what they need. He does it with less help, too. He estimates there are about 40 percent fewer people working this growing caseload than there were when he started five years ago. Hearing the stories of his fellow struggling Pittsburgh residents day in and day out, and knowing his own efforts to keep his family afloat, Levine finds himself perpetually amazed at the politicians who say he's to blame for the state's economic woes.

"The idea that somebody would say that the work I do is worth less . . ." He trails off, taking a second to mull the very thing he's heard for years from those who demonize public workers. "Does that mean I should make less and go out and find somewhere to sweep floors at night to make a few bucks more to make up for it? That I should be taken away from my child more than I am?"

Levine may be a nice guy, in a line of work whose very essence is taking care of those most in need. But he isn't a guy willing to be scapegoated and trampled by the conservatives in his own statehouse, or any statehouse for that matter.

"When I was six, we were driving by this coal company and there were mine workers picketing," Levine says. "I asked my mother about them and she told me these guys are union and they're fighting together. I remember that. I just knew you were supposed to support your union."

He's been an active AFSCME member for five years, and in the past two years he began speaking out more against the injustice he saw in his state and farther afield. Tell me why it's my fault, Levine thought every time he'd hear it. Show me how I'm the one screwing up. Instead, he did whatever he could to fight back online, reaching out to his networks of friends and family to talk about what was wrong with a law like Kasich's SB5. He watched with pride as he saw his union and others mobilize to fight in Wisconsin and Ohio. Cheered when the Wisconsin 14 left the state to prohibit passage of Walker's so-called budget repair bill. They were his fights, too.

On Ohio's election night, Levine watched from Pennsylvania for news of the vote against Issue 2. The future was at stake for his union brothers and sisters next door in the Buckeye State. And he knew, more than he ever acknowledged before the previous two years' attacks on public workers, that his own was, too. Levine scanned the crawl at the bottom of the television screen.

Victory.

"I felt like I owned a part of that win," Levine says. "I'm hopeful and proud of what was accomplished."

He adds one more thing. Something that should worry folks like Kasich and Walker about the affable guy from Pittsburgh.

"I'm fired up."

Back in Columbus, Ohio, Matthew De Voe, a zoo-keeper and father of three, was similarly elated when the results came on TV that night. "I am breathing a sigh of relief right now," said De Voe, who knew that if Issue 2 had passed, his life would have been turned upside down. "If this had

Courtesy of Tessa Berg

passed I might have lost my house. I looked at my kids the other night and had this fear that I wouldn't be able to provide for them. Tomorrow I can go back to work energized."

School-bus driver Karen Holdridge, who had knocked on hundreds of doors to collect petition signatures and then canvassed against Issue 2, couldn't stop smiling. "We did it. We

Courtesy of Tessa Berg

made history. I am so proud. We stood up and said, 'We are Americans and you cannot take our rights away.'"

And then there was BJ Simmons-Talley. When the reporter on the television screen at the election-night party she was attending announced news of the victory, BJ let out a cheer and began tearfully hugging anyone who came within reach. Here was the result of nearly a year of tireless effort to fight for workers' rights, by her and a team of thousands. She had vowed that we would not go back to a time before collective bargaining, to a time when workers weren't respected. And she had won. Reveling in the moment of victory, BJ threw up her arms, threw back her head, and hollered, "I am proud to be an Ohioan!"

We were proud of BJ.

CHAPTER TWELVE

From Madison to Manhattan

THE FIGHT FOR WORKERS' RIGHTS in Ohio and Wisconsin did more than bring labor issues to the forefront of public debate; it also shined a bright light on the growing chasm of income inequality in America that for decades has been largely ignored.

By 2011, that story was impossible to disregard, no matter how hard Fox News tried. There was a widening chasm splitting unevenly between the have-almost-everythings and the have-what-little-was-lefts.

By 2011, Americans knew there was a class war and the rich were winning.

They started paying more attention to news items that talked about how the six heirs to the Wal-Mart fortune held as much wealth as the entire bottom 30 percent of Americans. Or that the middle class was getting squeezed out of existence and there were numbers to prove it. Upward mobility was becoming more difficult. Americans had always believed that the next generation would do better than they themselves were doing. But

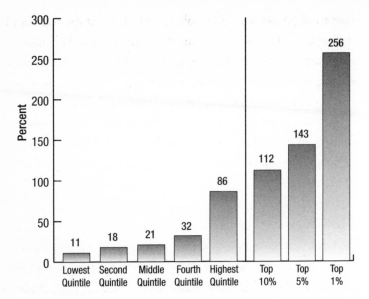

Increase in after-tax income by income group, 1979–2000

Source: Congressional Budget Office (2009).

now, economic projections started showing our children would be worse off than we were.

The facts were there.

From 1933 to 1979, average annual incomes in the United States grew by $38,000. The richest 10 percent of Americans got 30 percent of that growth. The rest of us took home 70 percent of it. Not too bad.

After 1979, the growth pattern flipped radically. From 1980 to 2008, our average income went up $11,714. The top tier got 98 percent of it. The average person got 2 percent.

Under President George H. W. Bush, average incomes actually declined by $1,912. The bottom 90 percent of Americans absorbed 72 percent of the blow, with those at the top shouldering the rest. Under his son, President George W. Bush, average income also went down, by $432. This time there was no sharing of the burden. Incomes didn't drop at all for the financial elite in the country. They shrunk for everybody else.[1]

By 2011, the top 1 percent of Americans took in nearly a quarter of the nation's income every year. In terms of overall wealth, not just income, the top 1 percent controlled 40 percent of the country's money.[2]

The United States for several years had been undergoing what policy wonks and economists call financialization. In that process, "financial markets, financial institutions, and financial elites gain greater influence over economic policy and economic outcomes" and it means that income is being made in America off of moving money around through the financial markets, not from producing actual goods like, say, a car or a washing machine. Added bonus—depending on what side of the chasm you were standing on—financialization exacerbates income inequality.[3]

As this was happening, the number of poor people in the country was growing. The rich were getting vastly richer. Corporations were accumulating record profits and sitting on piles of cash. A credit bubble was growing. People were making money from money, instead of from making things.

But there was no story. There was no catchphrase. Nothing to put on a bumper sticker.

Then came the crash of 2008.

The big banks had to be bailed out for sums that were unimaginable. We arrived there under the George W. Bush administration, following conservative policies of deregulation, yet the people most upset by the bailout were the true believers on the far right.

The response from the left, both to the crisis and to all that brought us to it, was that it was time to apply reason. The bailouts got more acceptance, however grudging, on the left than on the right. The bankers didn't deserve them, but it had to be done because otherwise a vast number of people who had nothing to do with the crisis would suffer. Now it was time for some reasonable regulations, like letting the unreasonable Bush tax cuts expire.

It turned out that reason was not enough.

The people with the greed, the big bankers, knew no shame. Gerald Celente, of the Trends Institute, calls them "money junkies." They took the bailout money—the public's money—and used it to pay lobbyists to keep themselves from being regulated. Then they paid themselves giant bonuses. It was no better over at insurance giant AIG. They got a $173 billion taxpayer bailout in late 2008. Six months later, in March 2010, they announced a plan to bestow $23 billion in holiday bonuses on some of the very traders responsible for collapsing the country's economy.

It was so egregious that even newspaper rivals *New York Daily News* and the *New York Post* agreed. The *Daily News* slammed A.I.G. IS A P.I.G. across its front page on March 17. The next day, as demand to block the bonuses grew, the Rupert Murdoch-owned *Post* gave its entire cover over to the headline NOT SO FAST YOU GREEDY BASTARDS.

Main Street was enraged with Wall Street.

Republican leaders in Congress meanwhile dedicated themselves to warfare against the Obama administration. They didn't even bother making it guerrilla warfare. United States Senate Minority Leader Mitch McConnell frequently announced to television cameras that the chief goal of Republicans was denying President Obama a second term.

We could take a glance at Congress's own bank accounts to see why it might not be identifying with the rest of us. The Center for Responsive Politics found last year that 47 percent of the members of Congress are millionaires. The estimated median net worth of a U.S. senator averaged $2.56 million.[4]

But Senator Bernie Sanders of Vermont was one of the few actually concerned about the poor and working class. So concerned, in fact, that he stood on the floor of the Senate for eight hours and thirty-seven minutes on December 10, 2010, filibustering a proposal to extend tax cuts for the rich and pass the country's financial burden onto the rest of us.

It was a little over a month since the Tea Party had swept into office, and its newly elected leaders were screaming the loudest in America, pledging to take on mythical overpaid public service workers as soon as they were let loose on Capitol Hill. (These were the same ideologues who would one day soon threaten to send the U.S. economy completely over the cliff by having the country default on its loans.)

But here was Senator Sanders, one man with one microphone, speaking out for those whose voices were increasingly being lost in all the shouting.

Sanders might have felt alone on the Senate floor, but someone was watching. A lot of folks, in fact. So many people tuned in on their computers to watch him speak that the Senate's video server crashed.[5]

America was starting to pay attention in late 2010.

In early 2011, the Wisconsin uprising reverberated across the country. American workers rose up in Ohio, in Indiana, in Tennessee, in Idaho. On *The Early Show,* CBS News reported that protesters gathered in all fifty states in support of the Wisconsin protesters and the working people being attacked within their own borders.[6]

Then came Bloombergville.

In June 2011, protesters began camping out in the park around New York's City Hall to rally against Mayor Bloomberg's budget cuts. Members of AFSCME District Councils 37 and 1707 helped organize it. Their statement of purpose:

> No library should close. No teacher or worker laid off. No tuition raised. No fire station closed. No unaffordable housing. And no social services ended.
>
> By increasing taxes on the wealthy and ending the wars and occupations the U.S. engages in, we could help those most affected by the budget cuts: working people, people of color, women, students, the homeless, among others. The solution is clear, and will only come from collective struggle.
>
> Bloombergville is an encampment to intensify and strengthen the struggle against austerity in New York City. It is a site of struggle and a community of resistance. We have drawn our inspiration from similar actions around the world, and we hope to inspire others.
>
> So long as austerity is on the agenda, we will be on the streets!

The protesters, including day care and Head Start providers, slept on the streets. Friends, family, and sympathetic New Yorkers brought them food. They cited their First Amendment rights to peacefully assemble. They were ordered to disperse. Some of them were arrested.

OCCUPY WALL STREET.

SEPTEMBER 17TH.

BRING TENT.

That was the mysterious, three-line invitation that the anti-commercial magazine *Adbusters* issued with posters in New York in early September. *Adbusters* got an assist from the online collective Anonymous and the group US Day of Rage.

On September 17 a couple of hundred folks arrived and set up their tents in Zuccotti Park, in the shadows of Wall Street and just five short blocks from City Hall.

What began as a modest group drawing curious stares from those hustling through the financial district grew quickly in the days to come. It wasn't the usual suspects—the young dread-locked and bandana-wearing anarchists who inevitably protested the World Trade Organization or the International Monetary Fund gatherings. To be sure, they were among them, but these were nurses, teachers, retirees, moms and dads pushing strollers, bus drivers, auto mechanics. They were standing up, in solidarity, and saying, "Enough!"

Television and cell-phone cameras alike swiveled to Wall

Street. Here was something concrete happening to protest the financial hell that had been unleashed on the vast majority of the country in recent decades. Here was the outgrowth of Wisconsin, of Ohio, of the Arab Spring. Here were men and women, students and senior citizens, public workers and private sector workers, the employed and the unemployed.

Here was the 99 percent.

WE ARE THE 99 PERCENT.

OCCUPY WALL STREET.

These were phrases that resonated the way previous attempts to reach the wider public, policy makers, and media alike hadn't. They concisely and vividly conveyed that 1 percent from Wall Street controlled the wealth in America and a full 99 percent of everyone else on Main Street were getting the short end of the stick, while simultaneously being beaten with it. These few words embodied downsizing, disappearing pensions, job loss, off-shoring and outsourcing, union busting, tax inequality, wage cuts, privatization, and the excess and injustice of vast wealth concentrated with a few.

At the same time, they offered hope. We're all in it together. The workers' uprising in Wisconsin was a call to action. The victory in Ohio proved that the people can win. This wasn't just about independent state battles anymore. It was the whole country.

WE ARE THE 99 PERCENT.

OCCUPY WALL STREET.

Those eight words belied a growing power. The movement they represented was starting to shift the national conversation about income inequality.

Conservatives had been dominating that conversation with hysterical cries about deficits, and the media willingly provided the microphone. The progressive blog *ThinkProgress* took a look at media coverage in the last week of July 2011 and found that the word "debt" was mentioned more than seven thousand times on MSNBC, CNN, and Fox News, and "unemployed" was only mentioned seventy-five times.[7]

In October, a month after Occupy Wall Street began, *ThinkProgress* took another look. The same three networks, between October 10 and October 16, used the word "debt" only 398 times. "Occupy" grabbed 1,278 mentions, "Wall Street" netted 2,378. The word falling most frequently from reporters' mouths now, at 2,738 mentions? "Jobs."

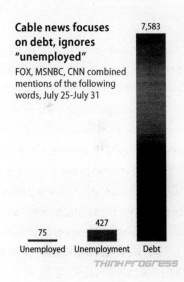

Cable news focuses on debt, ignores "unemployed"

FOX, MSNBC, CNN combined mentions of the following words, July 25-July 31

Unemployed	Unemployment	Debt
75	427	7,583

Source: This material (*Cable news focuses on debt, ignores "unemployed"*) was created by the Center for American Progress Action Fund (www.americanprogressaction.org).

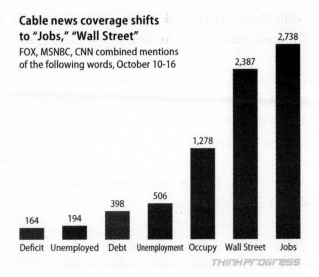

Cable news coverage shifts to "Jobs," "Wall Street"

FOX, MSNBC, CNN combined mentions of the following words, October 10-16

Deficit	164
Unemployed	194
Debt	398
Unemployment	506
Occupy	1,278
Wall Street	2,387
Jobs	2,738

THINKPROGRESS

Source: This material (*Cable news coverage shifts to "Jobs," "Wall Street"*) was created by the Center for American Progress Action Fund (www.americanprogressaction.org).

Also that fall, two studies about gaping income inequality got more attention than they likely would have ever garnered before Occupy Wall Street. The nonpartisan Congressional Budget Office revealed that the wealthiest 1 percent saw their incomes skyrocket 275 percent from 1979 to 2007. But 90 percent of households' income grew just 18 percent during that time. The Economic Policy Institute confirmed this troubling disparity in its own study.

WE ARE THE 99 PERCENT.

OCCUPY WALL STREET.

It's worth taking a closer look at what two very powerful, very wealthy men were saying as this revolution developed in America.

The first is GOP presidential hopeful Mitt Romney. In the summer of 2011, the former governor of Massachusetts and CEO of investment group Bain Capital, who was worth an estimated $250 million, traveled from primary contest to primary contest. In a stop at the Iowa State Fair, Romney uttered what would be the first of several revealing statements about the 1 percent versus the 99 percent that he'd make during the campaign. He told a man who was critical of his profit-above-all-else approach that "corporations are people, my friend." Some bystanders failed to contain their guffaws.

Then, in a nationally televised Republican presidential debate in Iowa, Romney offered fellow hopeful Texas Governor Rick Perry a $10,000 bet over the particular wording of something in a book he had written. "Ten thousand bucks?" he asked, casually extending his hand with the ease of one country-club goer challenging another on a golf outing. This time, the entire nation guffawed. (Not to be outdone, GOP hopeful Newt Gingrich would suggest in a later debate that poor children should replace paid janitors and clean their own schools.)

Finally, in February, Romney managed to top himself when it came to displaying rank insensitivity, telling a CNN reporter on camera, "I'm not concerned about the very poor." A man who was his party's front-runner for the presidency had just callously dismissed the plight of the most vulnerable in America.

This time, nobody was laughing.

That same summer of 2011 when Romney was busy scolding Iowa fair goers about corporations being regular folks, megabillionaire Warren Buffett was penning an opinion piece for the *New York Times*. In "Stop Coddling the Super-Rich," the chairman and chief executive of Berkshire Hathaway said it was nuts that he paid about 17 percent in income tax while staff members like his secretary Debbie paid an average of 36 percent.

His piece, which included the proposal that people making more than $1 million be taxed at a higher rate than those making a secretary's pay, instantly went viral. People shared it on social media as fast as their fingers could hit "like" and "retweet." It was dissected on cable news networks and blogs at similar lightning speed.

The second richest man in America, whose net worth hovered at $39 billion, had dropped a verbal bomb in the national conversation about income inequality. And he'd done it on behalf of the working class. His call for a tax rate more equitable to the 99 percent was dubbed "The Buffett Rule" and ultimately became a central part of President Obama's January 2012 State of the Union address.

During the State of the Union speech, Buffett's secretary Debbie sat with First Lady Michelle Obama as an honored guest.

CHAPTER THIRTEEN

This Is Our Moment

T HIS IS MAIN STREET'S MOMENT for a fresh economic and political vision. Rather, perhaps it's a *refreshing* vision, since it's one that includes some tried-and-true methods for realizing the American Dream, which we've allowed forty years of corporate-funded Lewis Powell–style hogwash to convince us didn't work.

It is a vision that works for 100 percent of us. Not just for those at the very top of the economic ladder. Not just for those who own oceanfront mansions and penthouse condos. For folks on Main Street—and your street.

We are talking about a patriotic vision that puts America first, not corporations. A vision that considers the economic health of our entire nation and won't accept hollowing out the middle class just so that billionaires can upgrade their private jets.

The phrases "Occupy Wall Street" and "We Are the 99 Percent" speak to the heart of the problem. The stranglehold on our economy by a very few has hurt our nation. There is nothing wrong with individuals getting rich. In the 1950s, when we weren't afraid to tax the wealthiest in the country, lots of people got rich. But economic prosperity was widespread. Wages and salaries rose across the board. We built roads and bridges and universities. We led the world in science and technology. And in job creation.

This is not a sentimental plea to return to "the good old days"—after all, the 1950s were also fraught with bigotry, sexism, segregation, and homophobia. But just as we have fought since then for civil rights, women's rights, and LGBT rights, we must fight now for economic rights.

We Are Ohio, the coalition of people from all walks of life that defeated Issue 2, reminded us that when we all pull together, we have the power to set things right. BJ Simmons-Talley in Ohio and LaTonya Johnson in Wisconsin and David Levine in Pennsylvania and every other proud American who stood up and said they'd had enough of economic injustice shows that Main Street can triumph. But for individual victories to drive national change, Main Street must make full use of this moment to do these things.

This Is Our Moment to Demand Good-Paying Jobs

Earlier in this book, LaTonya Johnson recalled moving in with her grandfather when she was twelve years old. "He took care of all of us. We thought he was rich. Now I understand, all he had was a good union job." We can and must make good-paying jobs the norm in America once again.

President Obama is on the right track with his proposed American Jobs Act, legislation that would invest in construction jobs for roads, waterways, and airports, modernize tens of thousands of schools, and prevent layoffs of hundreds of thousands of teachers and first responders.

Such common sense investment should be a no-brainer at a time when the president's record of success on jobs has been clear. Recall that when the president took office, the country was losing seven hundred thousand jobs a month. The American Recovery and Reinvestment Act stopped the bleeding and got us back into job creation mode. If there was one criticism of the act, it was that it wasn't enough. And unemployment lingered far too high for far too long.

But perhaps recognizing the president's accomplishments when it comes to jobs is precisely why his American Jobs Act has languished in Congress. None of the folks on TV news will mention it, but the truth is that the bosses on Wall Street and right-wing talk radio like high unemployment. It drives down wages and increases profits. That makes most corporate CEOs happy.

High unemployment also delights politicians like Senate Minority Leader Mitch McConnell. It makes President Obama look bad. You may recall that it was Senator McConnell who once said, "The single most important thing we want to achieve is for President Obama to be a one-term president." Not lower unemployment. Not help for families facing foreclosures. Not making sure that people like Dolores Bressette from Rhode Island can have a secure retirement. No, the single most important thing they want is to bring down the president of the United States.

If you understand that this is the guiding goal of corporate-backed politicians in Washington, D.C., much of their abysmal

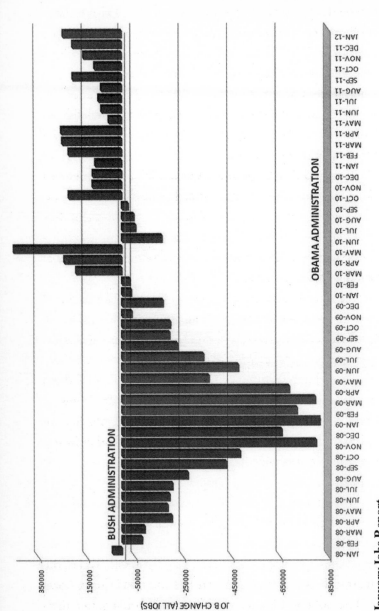

January Jobs Report

Source: Bureau of Labor Statistics, February 3, 2012.

record on the economy begins to make sense. It helps explain their efforts last spring, when the economy was beginning to recover, to launch an unprecedented months-long debate on whether the United States would increase the debt limit. They sent a clear message to the financial markets that the leadership in the U.S. House of Representatives was willing to risk the default of the United States rather than compromise on taxing the wealthiest people in America.

Never mind that this agenda hurts millions of America's working families. The House leadership in Washington may give lip service to the concerns of America's jobless, but they do what their bosses on Wall Street tell them to do. And that is: "Don't increase taxes on the rich." No wonder congressional approval is at historic lows.

It would be great if the free markets would whisk us out of our troubles without thought or effort, as if by an invisible hand, and we could each pursue our individual whims. But that's unlikely to happen. Just as we needed public investment to save the American automobile industry, only the heft of federal might is truly likely to lift us out of the economic doldrums.

This is our moment to demand good-paying jobs here in America, starting with the American Jobs Act and other incentives to bring jobs home.

This Is Our Moment for Shared Sacrifice

In 1955, the top marginal tax rate was 90 percent. Today, the top marginal tax rate for incomes near $400,000 is just 35 percent. The tax rate for *unearned* income, capital gains, dividends, and inheritances, is just 15 percent. And as we saw earlier, corporate tax loopholes have grown so large that General Electric didn't even owe taxes in 2010.

According to pro-corporate ideology, and former President Bush's stump speech as he tried to sell lowering taxes on the richest, all of this should have added up to more jobs than Americans knew what to do with and enough wealth should have trickled down that no one should want for anything. It was all a lie.

The giants of Wall Street and big business benefit from lower federal rates on capital gains, lower estate-tax rates, and other tax breaks beyond the reach of the middle class. Federal tax revenue is now at its lowest share of the economy since 1950.

For essentially the same reasons, state and local revenues, needed to pay for critical public services, also declined. That means bigger class sizes, crumbling roadways and bridges, and reneging on the promise of Social Security, all so that Mitt Romney can pay an obscenely low tax rate. Solving this very serious situation should be easy, but pro-corporate lawmakers have been willing to shut down their governments, or threaten equally dire measures, rather than raise one dollar more in taxes from their wealthiest constituents.

In July of 2011, the shutdown scenario played out dramatically in Minnesota, where more than twenty thousand state public employees were laid off for twenty days during a budget battle. This longest and largest layoff of public service workers in the state's history could have been avoided if lawmakers had agreed to create a tax system that deals fairly with corporations and the working middle class.

In an attempt to avoid the Minnesota debacle, Governor Mark Dayton offered a plan that hiked the tax rate for filers whose net income is more than $1 million per year—just 7,700 Minnesotans in all (0.3 percent of the state's population). But Tea Party lawmakers in the legislature rejected it. The deal that ultimately ended the shutdown failed to solve the state's long-term problems.

Getting out of the Great Recession will require shared sacrifice from all, not just working middle-class Americans who have seen their jobs evaporate and their incomes stagnate. Is the CEO of Sprint worth 227 special education teachers? Is Fox News media mogul Rupert Murdoch worth 420 police officers?

No.

And a corporate-raider-turned-politician isn't more valuable than a good nurse just because he has more money.

This is our moment to demand that the wealthiest Americans contribute their fair share again. Or, as Warren Buffett said in that *New York Times* piece, "It's time for our government to get serious about shared sacrifice."

This Is Our Moment to Protect Democracy

Lobbyists and corporate-owned politicians from both parties are fighting for the 1 percent. ALEC is writing laws that give them a few more millions when passed. They've got lawyers, professional union busters, private investigators, smear campaigns, threats, plant closings, public relations firms, advertising campaigns, lobbying, whatever it takes. The class war to elevate the 1 percent, to further inflate CEO pay and perks, to increase the power of corporations over people is being fought in the halls of government. And as we saw earlier, the 1 percent is winning.

It's not about left versus right. It's about right versus wrong.

And this has to be the moment when we say we value people over big money, just as we did in Wisconsin.

This has to be the moment when we win that argument, just as we did in Ohio.

Within the labor movement, private and public service workers must come together. As we have seen in Ohio and Wisconsin, when private and public service workers come together, we are a force to be reckoned with. We intend to keep those alliances alive.

But this isn't just about labor. Workers must join with students and parents to fight the privatization of education and ever-skyrocketing costs. Students must join with retirees to protect the promise of a retirement lived in dignity through pensions, Social Security, and Medicare. Retirees must join with working women to ensure equal pay for equal work.

Imagine the power of a coalition of the 99 percent.

While we're building this new coalition, let's talk about the role of money in our democracy. Whether we like it or not, politics has become an arms race, with money the weapon of choice. And even if we build a coalition of the 99 percent, corporate America will still outspend us. Those who gave the most money to anti-worker politicians in recent years got the most access. When Governor Scott Walker's citizens knocked on his door, he turned his back. When he thought billionaire bene-factor David Koch was calling, he picked up the phone.

You and I won't ever be able to give like a Koch brother can. But we can chip in two bucks a week.

At AFSCME, that's what our members pledge in order to support our political action committee, PEOPLE. That name is fitting, isn't it? Because while the new "super pacs" are bundling together millions from a handful of anonymous cor-porations, sanitation workers and nurses and office clerks are giving a few of their hard-earned dollars each week to help elect lawmakers who support fair taxation, retirement security, and saving the America Dream.

Never doubt that your donation of two dollars or two hun-dred dollars to a candidate or cause of your choice will make a difference. When President Obama was elected in 2008, it was thanks to some of the most democratic giving a campaign had ever spurred. Obama for America mobilized 3 million individ-uals who collectively gave $500 million. It came in the form of 6.5 million separate donations and most of them—6 million—were less than $100.

By joining their dollars together, Main Street elected a pres-ident. We can do it again.

Finally, protecting our democracy means protecting and expanding pro-democratic voices in the media. The United States of America is a country with more than 300 million peo-ple. On a typical evening, fewer than 2 million of them are watching Fox News. Yet the Murdoch-owned network has en-joyed a disproportionate amount of influence among media outlets since its earliest days.

Then came MSNBC.

Although the national television news outlets were slow to pick up on the scope of what was happening in Wisconsin, the sight of a hundred thousand in Madison sure woke them up. And once on the Wisconsin story, MSNBC in particular was willing to dive into the deep end of the pool on behalf of the people. Once upon a time, Fox News would have unilaterally marginalized the protesters, and ABC, NBC, and CBS would have offered little help explaining the issues on their shrinking news broadcasts. But the existence of MSNBC and the support of its most exuberant hosts—Al Sharpton, Ed Schultz, and Rachel Maddow in particular—was a game changer.

Night after night, on national television, they came back to the Wisconsin story with empathy and a clear understanding of what was at stake for working families. The images they broadcast, and the stories they told, humanized what was going on there and marked an important turning point in explaining to the country the significance of collective bargaining rights.

Now, we don't want to suggest that MSNBC was all by itself fighting the good fight. There were many print and radio journalists telling the story fairly and in depth. Steve Greenhouse and Monica Davey of the *New York Times* are two such reporters who quickly come to mind. Amy Goodman, John Nichols, Greg Sargent, Andy Kroll, and scores of progressive journalists from publications such as the *Nation, In These Times, American Prospect,* and *Mother Jones* were also doing terrific work.

But national television is national television, and its impact is still unparalleled. The folks who run MSNBC have made a decision to counter the right-wing programming zealotry of Rupert Murdoch and Fox News. As much as anything else, it is a business decision, a strategic move to gain an audience that wants to hear a progressive viewpoint.

It is a decision Main Street must embrace. Television networks live and die by ratings . If you don't watch, the format will change. And a huge opportunity will have been squandered. Main Street's chance to tell its story on national television each night will go dark.

Finally, sophisticated and often spontaneous use of social media like Facebook and Twitter is just as crucial as we move forward and spread the message. The pro-corporate propaganda machine is well oiled. A story appears on a major newspaper's website that is critical of unions and the "comments" section is flooded with virulent support. This doesn't happen by accident. You know the saying "If you see something, say something"? Well, that's what we need to do. When you read anti–Main Street pieces online, don't just get mad, get writing.

This Is Our Moment to Invest in the Public Good

How many times have you heard a politician or pundit on TV yelling that taxes suck money out of the economy? It makes us grab for the remote every time. The truth is that taxes provide revenue that keeps our economy working. Like aqueducts and reservoirs that redirect the flow of water to cities and towns and farms, government invests money in the public good, where it likely would not naturally flow.

There are certain things that simply have to be provided by government. Take national defense, for example. Let's say you and the two of us invest in national defense, but Mary, Bill, and Steve choose not to for whatever reason. They still get as much protection as the three of us. They can't be excluded from the benefits of our investment. That wouldn't be in the public interest.

This principle of the greater good, by the way, is the same reason we oppose so-called right-to-work laws. If everyone is getting the benefits of a union—higher wages, better health care, representation for grievances in the workplace—then everyone should contribute, even if they choose not to become members of the union. Otherwise, workers cede more and more to their bosses, or give up their standard of living entirely, which is the real goal of those who push such laws.

Like our national defense, government must ensure our environment is safe. We need clean air to breathe. Regulation of drugs and inspection of food, like the work Lee Eicher from Ohio does, are on the list, too. We must have universal education to ensure businesses have workers who can read and write, do math, and use computers.

There is a role for government in health care, too. When someone without health insurance goes to the emergency room, he or she isn't turned away and left to die. That's not in our value system as Americans, despite the fact that some people cheered the idea of a young man without insurance being left to die so that nobody had to pick up his medical tab, at one of last year's GOP presidential debates.

But the reality is that the cost of caring for the uninsured is passed along to those of us who are insured in the form of ever higher premiums. Some peg the cost at over $1,000 each year for Americans with insurance. That is the problem that the Affordable Care Act seeks to address by making sure that individuals take responsibility and purchase health insurance. The idea of such a mandate was pretty popular in conservative circles for quite some time. Mitt Romney made it a pillar of his health reform law as governor of Massachusetts. And Newt Gingrich supported the idea for years. Of course, that was before both men chose to run for president and decided to put politics above the public good.

The public good is served when tax dollars are invested in building roads, too. Public transportation systems—whether they are highways, subways, or bus routes—boost commerce. Goods can be shipped. People can arrive at work on time. And this can happen at minimal cost to the bottom line, whether it's a business ledger or a personal pocketbook.

If every roadway was privately funded, companies would focus on the areas where users with the ability to pay were driving. A lot fewer roads and bridges would get built. And a lot more would look like Indiana's toll road after Mitch Daniels privatized it. A family traveling the length of the toll road from Ohio to Illinois paid $4.65 in tolls in 2006 when the public was in charge. Today, if they don't have an electronic pass they pay $9.00 to the Macquarie Group and Cintra, two private investment companies based in Australia and Spain, respectively, which now have a seventy-five-year lease on the road.

If Scott Walker is the poster boy for a new breed of pro-corporate, anti-middle-class politicians, Mitch Daniels has been a poster child for privatization. In fact, he's earned the dubious nickname "Governor Privatize" for his willingness to stick a for sale sign on any public service he can. The results have been disastrous. Not only have prices on the toll road nearly doubled, but disruptions in vital public services have hurt the state's most vulnerable residents.

In 2006, Daniels contracted food stamp and Medicaid eligibility screening to IBM. The governor assured the public that laying off fourteen hundred public service workers and replacing them with an automated call center would boost efficiency.

The results were not pretty. Thousands of low-income Hoosiers were erroneously and cruelly dumped from the system. According to a story in the *Los Angeles Times* last year, an eighty-year-old woman from Terre Haute was dropped from her Medicaid payment "without warning when a private company took over the state's welfare system." She later learned the reason for being denied was her inability to call an eligibility hotline in 2008. The reason? She was in the hospital for congestive heart failure.[1]

In another case, a nun suffering from cancer was cut off from benefits, including food stamps, because she missed a re-certification interview with the company due to being hospitalized. She tried to reschedule her interview six times with IBM's call center and sent a fax. Her pleas were ignored.

In 2009, Indiana cancelled its billion dollar contract with IBM. Daniels did so after numerous reports of lost paperwork and records, long delays, and wrongly denied benefits. Indiana is now suing IBM for poor performance. But as *Business Week* reported in May 2010, IBM considers the state's allegations "unfounded" and blamed the service failures on the economic downturn that saw "benefits surging from 65,000 in March 2007, when IBM began its work, to nearly 120,000 during some months in 2008." According to IBM spokesperson Clint Roswell, "There were a number of assumptions made by the state in setting up this contract. One of them was that the economy would not lag."[2] Corporations will always tell taxpayers that they can do things better, faster, and cheaper than the public sector. But as Mr. Roswell demonstrates, it's important to read the fine print.

According to the *Los Angeles Times*, "Though the $1.37-billion project proved disastrous for many of the state's poor, elderly and disabled, it was a financial bonanza for a handful of firms with ties to Daniels and his political allies, which landed state contracts worth millions."[3]

Stories like this are plentiful in America today. They are the product of letting our politicians sell off public services to corporations that aren't accountable and simply don't care about the public good.

If this was the result in Indiana, imagine what would have happened had George W. Bush succeeded in 2005 with his scheme to privatize Social Security. Untold billions in retirement security would have been lost in the crash of 2008. An entire generation of retirees would have suddenly been faced with poverty in their golden years. And imagine what will happen if U.S. Representative Paul Ryan gets his way by privatizing Medicare, replacing the public-run program with a voucher system whereby seniors can purchase private insurance. Turning seniors' health care over to the profit-driven whims of the health insurance companies works just fine for people like Paul Ryan and Mitch Daniels. But not so well for the public at large.

The bottom line is this: too many times Main Street has been fleeced by corporations that say they can provide services better, faster, and cheaper than our government can. As Governor Privatize has shown us, and as we ponder the nightmare scenario that would have happened had we allowed George W. Bush to gamble away Social Security on the Wall Street casino, we must realize that selling off our public health, safety, education, and security to the highest corporate bidder does not serve the public good.

This Is Our Moment to Share in the Wealth That We Created Together

In pro-corporate ideology, the role of government should be as limited as possible. But the closer we get to eliminating government or shrinking it "down to the size where we can drown it in the bathtub," as Americans for Tax Reform's Grover Norquist once famously said he wanted to do, the worse the economy gets on Main Street.[4] We get bigger and bigger bubbles, with bigger crashes and bigger bank failures. All of which require bigger bailouts by everyone else—the 99 percent. And while the American worker is more and more productive, he and she get a smaller and smaller slice of the pie.

The pro-corporate politicians think this is just fine. They believe that the marketplace is self-correcting and self-stabilizing, truly guided by an invisible hand.

We spent a lot of time in this book documenting efforts of corporate-backed politicians to steal union rights. They did it in Wisconsin and tried to do it in Ohio because they knew that joining a union was one of the few ways Main Street can stand up and have a voice in how things are done in this country. But if we truly want to be heard, it's time we exercise our rights a little more.

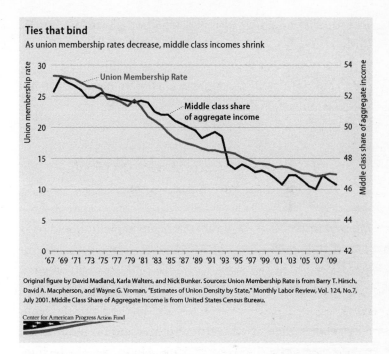

Ties that bind

As union membership rates decrease, middle class incomes shrink

Original figure by David Madland, Karla Walters, and Nick Bunker. Sources: Union Membership Rate is from Barry T. Hirsch, David A. Macpherson, and Wayne G. Vroman, "Estimates of Union Density by State," Monthly Labor Review, Vol. 124, No.7, July 2001. Middle Class Share of Aggregate Income is from United States Census Bureau.

Center for American Progress Action Fund

Source: This material (*Ties that bind*) was created by the Center for American Progress Action Fund (www.americanprogressaction.org).

Earlier we noted that as unions are strong, Main Street is strong. As Main Street is strong, the economy is solid and the country is strong. We even included a chart to prove it, a chart that summarizes this point so clearly that we figured we should show it again (see above).

There is no reason why we can't get organized to reverse this trend. There is no reason why Americans, the most productive and innovative people in the world, shouldn't be rewarded for their productivity and innovation by sharing in the wealth that we create together. There is no reason why you or anyone else can't take advantage of that promise of an extra $1,500 in your pocket. Let's get organized.

We believe that in America, if you work hard and play by the rules, you should earn a living wage. You should be able to afford health insurance. You should retire in dignity. You ought to be able to put your kids through school without saddling them with debt. We believe that we are at a pivotal moment in history when these American values must be protected. Throughout this book you have met some of the people on the front lines protecting them. Now is the moment for all Americans tired of being beaten down to stand together and join them.

Now is the moment to go to your state capitol and demand an end to assaults on people's voting rights.

Now is the moment to stand up at your city council or school board meeting to make sure corporations don't profit from hurting the public good.

Now is the moment to register to vote—and then register your friends, family, and neighbors.

This is Main Street's moment.

Let's get it done.

Notes

CHAPTER 1. MEET BETTY JEAN SIMMONS-TALLEY

1. Kasich for Ohio website, biography, http://www.kasich forohio.com/site/c.hpIJKWOCJqG/b.5280651/k.EB86/ Biography.htm.

2. John Kasich, *Stand for Something: The Battle for America's Soul* (New York: Grand Central Publishing), 61.

3. Landon Thomas Jr., "The Kasich Case: From Congressman to Businessman—John Kasich Cuts a New Deal," *New York Observer*, September 17, 2001, http://www.observer.com/ 2001/09/the-kasich-case-from-congressman-to-businessman -john-kasich-cuts-a-new-deal/.

4. Ibid.

5. Steve Fishman, "Burning Down His House," *New York* magazine, http://nymag.com/news/business/52603/.

6. "Who Deserves the Most Blame?," *Time* Specials, February 11, 2009, http://www.time.com/time/specials/packages/ article/0,28804,1877351_1878509_1878508,00.html.

7. Thomas, "The Kasich Case."

8. Jon Hallet, "Kasich made more than $1 million in 2008, tax returns show" *Columbus Dispatch*, April 2, 2010, http://

www.dispatch.com/content/stories/local/2010/04/02/kasich
-releases-2008-tax-returns.html.

9. Douglas McIntyre, "The Layoff Kings," *Daily Finance,*
August 18, 2010, http://www.dailyfinance.com/2010/08/18/
the-layoff-kings-the-25-companies-responsible-for-700-000-
lost/.

10. Strickland campaign press release. See "Public Records
Requests Show Kasich Campaign Repeatedly Dishonest," February 5, 2012, http://newsdemocrat.com/main.asp?SectionID
=219&SubSectionID=1375&ArticleID=131315.

11. Kasich, *Stand for Something,* 2–3.

CHAPTER 2. SPECIAL OFFER TO OUR READERS—
$1,500 A YEAR, FOR LIFE

1. "Daniels RTW" video clip, http://www.youtube.com/
watch?v=lPgxYa-rdmg. Uploaded by inlabor 2010 on January
19, 2010.

2. David Madland, Karla Walter, and Nick Bunker, "Unions
Make the Middle Class: Without Unions, the Middle Class Withers," Center for American Progress Action Fund, April 4, 2011.

3. Robert C. Johansson, Jay S. Coggins, and Benjamin
Senauer, "Union Density Effects in the Supermarket Industry,"
August 1999, University of Minnesota, http://purl.umn.edu/
14313.

4. According to the Congressional Budget Office (cbo.
gov/doc.cfm?index=12118), $432 billion was employed in the
Troubled Asset Relief Program (TARP), although $700 billion
was authorized. According to Bloomberg News, the fed loaned

out $7.77 trillion on top of that with interest rates of nearly zero. Since they were below market rates, that allowed the banks that got the free federal money to make $13 billion in profits. See http://www.bloomberg.com/news/2011-11-28/secret-fed -loans-undisclosed-to-congress-gave-banks-13-billion-in -income.html.

5. Ben Bernanke, speech before the Omaha Chamber of Commerce, February 6, 2007, http://www.federalreserve.gov/ newsevents/speech/bernanke20070206a.htm.

6. Madland, "Unions Make the Middle Class."

7. A PDF of the study is available at http://www.npc.umich .edu/news/events/bruce-western/union02.pdf.

8. Http://www.mybudget360.com/does-a-college-degree- protect-your-career-unemployment-rate-for-college-graduates- highest-on-record/.

9. Jennifer Lee, "Generation Limbo," *New York Times,* August 31, 2011, http://www.nytimes.com/2011/09/01/fashion/ recent-college-graduates-wait-for-their-real-careers-to-begin .html?pagewanted=all.

10. Betsy Stark, "Discouraged College Graduates Drop- ping Out of Workforce 'in Droves,' Says Study," ABC News, February 25, 2010, http://abcnews.go.com/Business/jobs -recent-college-graduates-discouraged-students-leaving- workforce/story?id=9933402#.TuOIgopiYoc.

CHAPTER 3. CLASS WARFARE

1. Ben Stein, "In Class Warfare, Guess Which Class Is Win- ning?" *New York Times*, November 26, 2006.

2. Kirsten Powers, "To Romney, Detractors Suffer from Envy," *Daily Beast,* www.thedailybeast.com/articles/2012/01/13/to-romney-detractors-suffer-from-envy.html.

3. Michael Smerconish program, October 6, 2011.

4. Radley Glasser and Steve Rendall, "For Media, 'Class War' Has Wealthy Victims: Rich Retting Richer Seldom Labeled as Belligerents," August 2009, http://www.fair.org/index.php?page=3846.

5. Ibid.

6. Jim Wallis, "God and Class Warfare," *Huffington Post,* September 22, 2011, http://www.huffingtonpost.com/jim-wallis/god-and-class-warfare_b_976403.html.

7. Claudia Goldin and Robert A. Margo, "The Great Compression: The Wage Structure in the United States at Mid-Century," 1992. A PDF of the paper may be accessed at http://www.nber.org/papers/w3817.pdf.

8. Henry M. Wachtel, *Street of Dreams—Boulevard of Broken Hearts: Wall Street's First Century* (London: Pluto Press, 2003).

9. This and following quotes are from the memorandum, a typescript of which can be found at http://law.wlu.edu/dept images/Powell%20Archives/PowellMemorandumTypescript.pdf.

10. Kim Phillips-Fein, *Invisible Hands: The Making of the Conservative Movement from the New Deal to Reagan* (New York: W. W. Norton, 2009), 169.

11. Ibid., 162.

12. Eric Lipton, Mike Mcintire, and Don Van Natta Jr., "Top Corporations Aid U.S. Chamber of Commerce Campaign," *New York Times,* October 21, 2010.

CHAPTER 4. CLASS WARRIORS:
THE KOCH BROTHERS AND ALEC

1. Jane, Mayer, "Covert Operations: The Billionaire Brothers Who Are Waging a War against Obama," *New Yorker,* August 30, 2010, http://www.newyorker.com/reporting/2010/08/30/100830fa_fact_mayer?currentPage=all.

2. Greenpeace, "Koch Industries Still Fueling Climate Denial: 2011 Update," April 14, 2011, http://www.greenpeace.org/usa/en/campaigns/global-warming-and-energy/polluter watch/koch-industries/.

3. Forbes.com, "#2 Koch Industries," http://www.forbes.com/lists/2011/21/private-companies-11_Koch-Industries_VMZQ.html.

4. Koch Industries website, http://www.kochind.com.

5. Mayer, "Covert Operations."

6. KochFacts.com, "Koch Seminars," August 5, 2011, http://www.kochfacts.com/kf/koch_seminars/.

7. Brad Friedman, "Exclusive Audio: Inside the Koch Brothers' Secret Seminar," *Mother Jones,* September 6, 2011, http://motherjones.com/politics/2011/09/exclusive-audio-koch-brothers-seminar-tapes.

8. Kate Zernike, "Secretive Republican Donors Are Planning Ahead," *New York Times,* October 19, 2010, http://www.nytimes.com/2010/10/20/us/politics/20koch.html.

9. Ibid.

10. The Brad Blog, http://www.bradblog.com/?page_id=8700.

11. Mayer, "Covert Operations."

12. The story is from the *Wall Street Journal*, but it's been

proudly placed on the Mercatus website: http://mercatus.org/
media_clipping/rule-breaker-washington-tiny-think-tank-
wields-big-stick-regulation.

13. Kenneth P. Vogel and Ben Smith, "Koch Brothers Plans
for 2010," *Common Dreams,* February 11, 2012, http://www.
commondreams.org/headline/2011/02/11-1.

14. John Biewen, "Corrections, Inc.: Part I—Corporate-
Sponsored Crime Laws," American RadioWorks, April 2002,
http://www.americanradioworks.org/features/corrections/
index.html.

15. "ALEC: Ghostwriting the Law for Corporate America,"
American Association for Justice, http://www.justice.org/cps/rde//
justice/hs.xsl/15044.htm.

16. Common Cause press release, "Common Cause Seeks
Audit of Corporate/Legislative Group," July 14, 2011, http://
www.commoncause.org/site/apps/nlnet/content2.aspx?c=dk
LNK1MQIwG&b=810365&ct=10902603.

17. Merle Travis, "Sixteen Tons," *Folk Songs of the Hills,*
Bear Family, 1947, compact disc. Or by George Davis, who
claims to have written it earlier, but recorded it later, *When Kentucky Had No Union Men,* Smithsonian Folkways, 2010, compact disc. Originally released in 1967.

18. http://www.economicpopulist.org/content/which-side
-are-you.

19. Report of the Commission appointed by Kentucky
Governor Ruby Laffoon, June 6, 1935, quoted various places
including the *Palm Beach Post,* June 7, 1935.

20. Shauna L. Scott, *Two Sides to Everything: The Cultural
Construction of Class Consciousness in Harlan County* (Albany:
State University of New York Press, 1995), 28.

21. Alessandro Portelli, *They Say in Harlan County: An Oral History* (New York, Oxford University Press, Nov 10, 2010), 189.

22. The average credit card rate, Christmas week 2011, http://www.bankrate.com/finance/news/credit-cards/interest-rates-122211.aspx.

23. Blake Ellis, "The Average Student Loan Debt Tops $25,000," CNNMoney, http://money.cnn.com/2011/11/03/pf/student_loan_debt/index.htm.

CHAPTER 6. THE LAST LINE OF DEFENSE

1. *Congressional Digest*, Federal Labor Laws, June–July 1993, accessed at: http://history.eserver.org/us-labor-law.txt.

2. Ibid.

3. James C. Klotter, *Kentucky: Portrait in Paradox, 1900–1950* (Frankfort, KY: Kentucky Historical Society, 2006), 143.

4. Ibid.

5. Harry S. Truman radio address on the veto of the Taft-Hartley Bill, June 20, 1947. Accessed at http://millercenter.org/president/speeches/detail/3344.

6. D&S Collective, "The Economics of the Air Controllers' Strike," *Dollars & Sense*, October 1981, http://www.dollarsand sense.org/archives/1981/1081patco.html.

7. Remarks by Chairman Alan Greenspan: The Reagan Legacy, April 9, 2003, Ronald Reagan Library, Simi Valley, California, http://www.federalreserve.gov/boarddocs/speeches/2003/200304092/default.htm#pagetop.

8. Kathleen Schalch, "1981 Strike Leaves Legacy for Amer-

ican Workers," NPR, August 3, 2006, http://www.npr.org/templates/story/story.php?storyId=5604656.

9. Ibid.

10. Http://www.oup.com/us/catalog/general/subject/HistoryAmerican/?view=usa&ci=9780199836789.

11. Ibid.

12. Steven Greenhouse, *The Big Squeeze: Tough Time for the American Worker* (New York: Knopf, 2008), 81–82.

13. Jerry Wurf, *Labor's Last Angry Man*, Goulden, Joseph C. AFSCME, 1982, 2.

14. Ibid., 29.

15. Theodore Roosevelt speech, "The New Nationalism," August 31, 1910, at the dedication of the John Brown Memorial State Park in Osawatomie, Kansas.

CHAPTER 7. MEET SCOTT WALKER

1. Adam Weinstein, "Did Gov. Scott Walker Pull a Tracy Flick?," *Mother Jones,* February 19, 2011, http://motherjones.com/mojo/2011/02/scott-walker-tracy-flick-wisconsin-school-election.

2. Editorial, *Marquette Tribune*, February 24, 1988.

3. *Marquette Tribune*, February 24, 1988. The first time was on the 23rd, Walker's people stole copies, so it was reprinted on Wed. 24th with the additional information.

4. John Biewen, "Corrections, Inc."

5. Ibid.

6. Patrick Marley, "Walker Says He Would Cut Taxes in

First Budget," *All Politics Blog*, http://www.jsonline.com/blogs/news/68643847.html#comments.

7. Jeffrey H. Keefe, "Are Wisconsin Public Employees Over-Compensated?" Economic Policy Institute, February 10, 2011, http://www.epi.org/publication/are_wisconsin_public_employees_over-compensated/.

8. "Fitzgerald Inc. Reveals GOP Plans for a 'Right to Work' Wisconsin," video clip, https:www.youtube.com/watch?v=dzs _ZMUvS_w. Video footage uploaded by wisdems09 on December 9, 2010.

CHAPTER 8. THE REAL AGENDA

1. Mary Bottari, "ALEC Bills in Wisconsin" PR Watch, Center for Media and Democracy, July 14, 2011, http://www.prwatch.org/news/2011/07/10880/alec-bills-wisconsin.

2. Erin Richards and Amy Hetzner, "Choice Schools Not Outperforming MPS," *Milwaukee Journal Sentinel,* March 29, 2011, http://www.jsonline.com/news/education/118820339.html.

3. Patrick Marley and Jason Stein, "Walker Signs Budget Bill, Vetoes Just 50 Items," *Milwaukee Journal Sentinel,* June 26, 2011, http://www.jsonline.com/news/statepolitics/124563073.html.

4. Video clip by *Morning Joe*, August 12, 2011. Accessed at http://www.bing.com/videos/watch/video/gov-walker-ill-be-judged-by-my-job-creation-record/6kabmz5?cpkey=11537a82-8aee-420e-9587-6cc1f85c4ed6.

5. "Wisconsin Led Nation in Jobs Lost in November," *Biz-Times Daily*, December 20, 2011, http://www.biztimes.com/daily/2011/12/20/wisconsin-led-nation-in-jobs-lost-in-november.

6. John Schmid, "Wisconsin Lost 3,900 Private-Sector Jobs in December," *Milwaukee Journal Sentinel*, January 19, 2012, http://www.jsonline.com/business/wisconsin-lost-3900-privatesector-jobs-in-december-s33s7b4-137686343.html.

7. "Year in Review: Wisconsin Closes 2011 with Six Straight Months of Job Loss," Center on Wisconsin Strategy, http://www.cows.org/pdf/ds-WIJobWatch-Dec11.pdf.

8. Federal Reserve Bank of Philadelphia website, "State Co-incident Indexes," February 12, 2012, http://www.philadelphia fed.org/research-and-data/regional-economy/indexes/coincident/.

9. "Transcript of Prank Koch-Walker Conversation," *Wisconsin State Journal*, February 23, 2011, http://host.madison .com/wsj/article_531276b6-3f6a-11e0-b288-001cc4c002e0 .html#ixzz1k3cSGGLl.

CHAPTER 9. ON, WISCONSIN!

1. Press release, "Conservatives, Republicans Call Radical Scheme 'Anti-Freedom,' 'Big Government Power Grab Against Individual Rights,'" February 14, 2011.

2. Peter Rickman, private notes.

3. Ibid.

4. *AFSCME Works,* Spring 2011, http://www.afscme.org/news/publications/newsletters/works/pdf/Works-Spring2011 .pdf.

5. Ibid.

6. "We Have a Fire in the House of Labor," *Democracy Now!*, February 21, 2011, http://www.democracynow.org/2011/2/21/we_have_a_fire_in_the.

CHAPTER 10. THE BUCKEYE BARRAGE

1. John Guillen, "Ohio Senate Republicans Pass Collective Bargaining Overhaul by Narrowest Margin," *Plain Dealer*, March 2, 2011, http://www.cleveland.com/open/index.ssf/2011/03/ohio_senate_republicans_pass_c.html.

2. "OH: Seitz," video clip, http://www.youtube.com/watch?v=hxK7-Vg1YcU. Uploaded by mrcawguy, May 1, 2011.

3. "SB 5: Did the Speaker Really Say That?" Politics Extra blog, *Cincinnati Enquirer,* April 1, 2011, http://cincinnati.com/blogs/politics/2011/04/01/sb-5-did-the-speaker-really-say-that/.

4. John M. Spinelli, "Gallery Chants 'Shame on You,'" *Columbus Government Examiner*, March 30, 2011, http://www.examiner.com/government-in-columbus/gallery-chants-shame-on-you-after-ohio-house-passes-sb5-by-53-44-vote.

5. *The Ed Show*, MSNBC 10/26/2011. "Ohio Right-Wing Talk Show Host Takes Position against Anti-Collective-Bargaining Law," *Washington Independent,* October 31, 2011, http://washingtonindependent.com/114894/ohio-right-wing-talk-show-host-takes-position-against-anti-collective-bargaining-law.

6. "Think Again: Taking Back Ohio," video clip, http://

www.youtube.com/watch?v=fSFhy-JU4cU&feature=player_ embedded. Uploaded by AFSCME on November 9, 2011.

7. Joe Vardon, Joe Hallett, and Tristan Navera, "Money Rains, Rallies Rock in Issue 2 Slugfest," *Columbus Dispatch*, November 4, 2011, http://www.dispatch.com/content/stories/local/2011/11/04/money-rains-rallies-rock-in-issue-2-slugfest.html.

8. David Blaska, "R.I.P. Wisconsin Government Employee Unions," *Daily Page,* February 9, 2011, http://www.thedaily page.com/daily/article.php?article=32170.

CHAPTER 11. VICTORY IN OHIO

1. "'Marlene Quinn & Zoey'—Vote NO on Issue 2," video clip, http://www.youtube.com/watch?v=zQnEZGaSqD4. Uploaded by WeAreOhio on October 6, 2011.

2. Reginald Fields, "Television Stations Pulling SB5 Commercial over Concerns It Is Misleading," *Plain Dealer,* October 12, 2011, http://www.cleveland.com/open/index.ssf/2011/10/television_stations_pulling_sb.html.

3. Jim Siegel, "Recut Television Ad Makes SB5 Look Like a Supporter," *Columbus Dispatch*, October 13, 2011, http://www.dispatch.com/content/stories/local/2011/10/12/recut-television-ad-turns-sb-5-opponent-into-backer.html#.

4. Press release, "'Yes on Issue 2': Campaign Sinks to New Low," http://weareohio.com/news/pr/101111.html.

5. "Think Again: Taking Back Ohio."

CHAPTER 12. FROM MADISON TO MANHATTAN

1. All averages from the Economic Policy Institute, http://stateofworkingamerica.org/who-gains/#/?start=2001&end=2008.

2. Joseph Stiglitz, "Of the 1%, by the 1%, for the 1%," *Vanity Fair*, May 2011.

3. Thomas I. Palley, "Financialization: What It Is and Why It Matters," Working Paper No. 525, Levy Economics Institute, and Economics for Democratic and Open Societies, December 2007, http://www.levyinstitute.org/publications/?docid=971.

4. Tom Shine, "47 Percent of Congress Members Millionaires," *Note*, November 16, 2011, http://abcnews.go.com/blogs/politics/2011/11/47-of-congress-members-millionaires-a-status-shared-by-only-1-of-americans/.

5. Nick Wing, "Bernie Sanders Filibuster: Senator Stalls Tax Cut Deal," *Huffington Post*, December 10, 2010, http://www.huffingtonpost.com/2010/12/10/bernie-sanders-filibuster_n_795087.html.

6. "Rallies in 50 States Support Wis. Protesters," *The Early Show,* CBS News, February 26, 2011. See http://www.cbsnews.com/stories/2011/02/26/earlyshow/saturday/main20036739.shtml.

7. Zaid Jilani, "Thanks to the 99 Percent Movement, Media Finally Covering Jobs Crisis j Marginalizing Deficit Hysteria," *ThinkProgress,* October 18, 2011, http://thinkprogress.org/special/2011/10/18/346892/chart-media-jobs-wall-street-ignoring-deficit-hysteria/.

CHAPTER 13. THIS IS OUR MOMENT

1. "Indiana's Bumpy Road to Privatization," *Los Angeles Times,* June 24, 2011,http://articles.latimes.com/2011/jun/24/nation/la-na-indiana-privatize-20110624.

2. "Indiana Agency, IBM Sue Each Other over $1.3B Deal," *Bloomberg Businessweek,* May 13, 2010, http://www.businessweek.com/ap/financialnews/D9FM5E580.htm.

3. "Indiana's Bumpy Road to Privatization."

4. Grover Norquist, SourceWatch, http://www.sourcewatch.org/index.php?title=Grover_Norquist.

Index

About the Authors

Gerald W. McEntee is the president of the 1.6 million-member American Federation of State, County and Municipal Employees, AFL-CIO (AFSCME). First elected AFSCME president in 1981, he has transformed AFSCME into one of the most aggressive and politically active organizing unions in the country. He is chairman of the AFL-CIO's Political Education Committee and was a leader in the successful fights to protect Social Security during the second Bush presidency and to pass health care reform in the Obama years. A native of Philadelphia, McEntee and his wife, Barbara, live in Washington, D.C.

Lee Saunders is the secretary-treasurer of the American Federation of State, County and Municipal Employees, AFL-CIO (AFSCME). Saunders began his career working for the Ohio Bureau of Employment Services in 1974 and is now one of the highest ranking African Americans in the labor movement. He serves as a vice president of the AFL-CIO, treasurer of the Leadership Conference on Civil and Human Rights, and as a member of the board of the National Action Network. Saunders and his wife, Lynne, live in Washington, D.C.